CACTI
SUCCULENTS

190

1992

CACTI & SUCCULENTS

Clive Innes

WARD LOCK LIMITED · LONDON

ACKNOWLEDGEMENTS

The publishers gratefully acknowledge Holly Gate Nurseries Ltd in granting permission to reproduce all colour photographs.

All the line drawings were drawn by Nils Solberg.

Front cover: *Echinopsis oxygona multiplex,* courtesy Pat Brindley.

First published in Great Britain in 1988
by Ward Lock Limited, 8 Clifford Street
London W1X 1RB, an Egmont Company

House editor Denis Ingram
Text set in Bembo by
Hourds Typographica, Stafford

Printed and bound in Portugal by Resopal

British Library Cataloguing in Publication Data
Innes, Clive
　　Cacti and other succulent plants.
　　1. Cactus
　　I. Title
　　635.9'3347　　　　SB478
　　ISBN 0–7063–6628–X

Cover: *Heliocereus speciosus* var. *superbus*.

Frontispiece: *Aloe humilis* is a free-flowering species with its elegant spike arising direct from a most compact rosette of sharply pointed leaves.

CONTENTS

PREFACE

Many thousands of people around the world have become involved with collecting and growing cacti and succulents. This is at the least a fascinating hobby and once infatuation has taken hold the wonder of it all rarely ceases to attract. It is essential to learn to differentiate between a true cactus and so called 'other' succulents. Far too many plants are dubbed 'cactus' just because they look different. Cacti *do* look different, but so do other succulents.

Succulent plants are to be found in more than 500 different genera, well over 150 of which belong to the family Cactaceae. A great deal of botanical research has taken place in recent years and is continuing. As a result, cactus nomenclature has gone through many upheavals and is still changing. Many genera have been merged with others, so many well-known names like *Zygocactus*, *Lemaireocereus* and *Trichocereus* have become obsolete. These changes have been taken into account in this book.

Correct nomenclature is vital – certainly for the beginner and even more for the knowledgeable enthusiast – since it provides the only way in which one can get the facts about a species. The Latin name is the key to authoritative and often original works in which you can find full descriptive details. Hence no common names are mentioned here, since they can refer to one or several plants, possibly even in different genera.

Cacti and succulents are closely akin as both can withstand long periods of drought by storing water and nourishment in their stems, leaves or rootstock. They can therefore survive when most other plants would succumb. This book provides adequate guidance to identifying and understanding these plants. Though it describes only a limited number of representative species, these are generally considered very attractive and reasonably easy to grow successfully, and they are available from many garden centres and succulent plant nurseries. Practical advice is also given about cultivation and keeping the plants healthy and growing well.

As an enthusiast for many years, I would recommend this hobby as one of the most intriguing. It can bring endless pleasure and, as you become more deeply involved, happy and even magnificent surprises.

Ashington, West Sussex.

C. I.

PART I
GENERAL

CHAPTER I

THE GEOGRAPHICAL DISTRIBUTION OF SUCCULENT PLANTS

Succulent plants are to be found in almost every part of the world, from the near Arctic regions, throughout tropical, sub-tropical and equatorial areas, and in fact nearly everywhere that adverse climatic conditions prevail. Scarcity of space makes it necessary to generalize to an extent, the more so as certain species within specific genera are discovered in varying and extreme temperature areas.

AMERICA

Geographically, all cacti are native to the New World, and whilst *apparently* wild species are to be found in many parts of the world where conducive weather conditions enable plants to grow out-of-doors – such as southern parts of Europe, Australia and South Africa – their real home is centred in the Americas, from southern parts of Canada to the south of Argentina. This wide distribution of genera and species emphasizes the capabilities of these plants to tolerate many unpleasant conditions, both of heat and cold. Obviously what grows in the hotter regions will not survive if confronted with extreme cold; this frequently is the lot of those from northern parts of America. The wisest course is always to strike a happy medium in cultivation. This is why it is usually recommended that cacti should not be allowed to become frosted and, as far as possible, to maintain a minimum temperature of 7–10°C (45–50°F) at all times, and in the coldest months to allow plants to rest by withholding moisture.

There is a section of the Cactaceae family which is totally epiphytic in its natural habitat – particularly *Epiphyllum*, sometimes known as the orchid cactus; Christmas and Easter cacti, which are now considered to be species of *Schlumbergera* and *Rhipsalidopsis* respectively; and *Rhipsalis*, and certain of the climbing, clambering species of *Selenicereus* and *Hylocereus*. Such plants occur principally from Central Mexico to more southerly areas of Brazil and many of the West Indian islands. Rain forests are mainly their home; invariably they flower and grow during the period of the European winter, so warmer temperatures must be guaranteed of nothing less than 10°C (50°F). This will enable plants to flourish and bloom at a time when other cacti are flowerless and dormant.

There are certainly succulent plants other than cacti to be found in the New World: *Agave*, *Echeveria*, *Yucca*, *Sedum* are representative of genera frequently encountered. Once again, many species withstand very low temperatures; some have in fact become well established in parts of Britain as garden plants, although it must be borne in mind that they require planting in a protected, south-facing position.

EUROPE

Some species of the Crassulaceae are endemic to parts of Europe, including Britain. Stonecrop is a very well known species of the *Sedum* genus. The southern Alps and the Pyrenees are the natural home of the *Sempervivum*, many species and cultivars of which have found their way into general cultivation. Further south into Spain and Portugal different species of *Sedum* grow, mostly in mountainous areas, and one or two genera of the Asclepiadaceae, notably *Caralluma*. The islands of the Canaries and Madeira are home to many desirable succulents. Here is the principal habitat of the genus *Aeonium*, also of the family Crassulaceae, together with some of the family Asclepiadaceae including many *Ceropegia* with their unusual, lantern-like flowers.

AFRICA

The whole continent of Africa abounds in succulent plants which are included within some of the largest of plant familes – Mesembryanthe-maceae, Euphorbiaceae and Liliaceae – the latter so well represented by *Aloe*, *Haworthia* and *Gasteria* which might be termed bulbless lilies. Asclepiadaceae includes many well-known genera, undoubtedly the best known being *Stapelia*, one species of which, *Stapelia variegata*, now known under a new generic title of *Orbea variegata*, is referred to as the carrion flower due to its obnoxious smell; yet it has an attractive flower! Once again, temperature conditions and climate change considerably in such a vast land coverage. Whilst most of the Liliaceae provide little diffi-culty in cultivation, being happily responsive to much the same cultiva-tion requirements as most cacti, others, especially those of Asclepiadaceae require more specialized attention, particularly in relation to humidity as they can so easily rot. The Mesembryanthemums are certainly less difficult so long as the individual needs of the genus are observed, i.e. the growing and resting periods or when to water, and when to keep dry. They will prove fascinating, floriferous and generally rewarding plants if it is remembered that a minimum temperature of 10°C (50°F) is necessary. More detail will be given about some of these when particular species are described. Euphorbias, especially the South African species, are relatively easy to cultivate. They are frequently encountered in close proximity with Aloes, and in general will respond to much the same treatment. Of all succulents, many species of *Euphorbia* are erroneously thought to be cacti – the unusual shapes of some do have their counterparts within the Cactaceae!

The major geographical distribution has been considered, but many other important areas deserve mention. Australasia and Asia have many species endemic to both arid and jungle regions. Possibly one of the the better known genera represented in both continents is *Hoya*, commonly known as the wax flower, and this, together with many other twining or bushy species, is succulent, adapting itself readily to greenhouse or home culture. Cacti and succulents, wherever their origin, will respond to comfortable conditions and attention. Heat is not essential to success, but warmth definitely is, and not too much cold.

AUSTRALIA

This vast continent boasts of several important and extraordinary succulents, most of them in genera unknown elsewhere. The outstanding *Xanthorrhoea*, known locally as Blackboys, includes species of particular significance. Likewise a few succulent *Hoya* are native to the rain-forest areas of Queensland. The splendid array of Australian succulents has not been widely distributed in collections, but seeds are becoming more readily available. Propagation of these plants poses no greater problems than those from other continents.

The well-known *Aloe variegata* has never lost its popularity for both greenhouse and home culture, but good light is an essential.

CHAPTER 2

THE PRINCIPAL CHARACTERISTICS

CACTI

So often the question arises what the difference is between a cactus and other succulent plants. Fundamentally, the important query to answer is – what is a cactus? The name is derived from the Greek *kaktos* meaning a 'prickly plant'. It is, of course, untrue that all plants with prickles are cacti. Many such species are also to be found in other succulent plant genera.

All cacti are true succulents but have certain characteristics not in evidence elsewhere in the world of plants. Cacti are dicotyledons; this means to say that when the seed germinates it develops two leaf-like growths, from the centre of which emerges the minute cactus seedling. All species are perennials and it is not uncommon for plants to take several years before reaching flowering stage. Unlike annuals, where seeds germinate, grow to maturity and flower all in one season, cacti develop slowly and generally require more than one year before flowers appear, but there are exceptions! The main characteristics can be summarised as follows:

1 Regardless of their shape or size, all cacti – globular, columnar, pad-shaped or leaf-like – possess a peculiar growing point called an 'areole'. It may not be apparent on some species, but usually it shows as a small round or elongated cushion consisting of woolly felt or bristly hairs. In certain species, such as *Opuntia*, the small hairs of the areole are referred to as glochids which readily become detached by the touch of the hand, and many cause irritation to the skin. The areole actually incorporates two growing points, these often being set close together so they appear as one. The areole then develops spines from the lower part, and the flower bud and 'branches' from the upper. This botanically is one of the most important features of the Cactaceae, and it is essential that this distinctive characteristic is emphasized.

2 The flower is always set *above* the ovary or 'fruit'.

3 The fruit or seed-pod is botanically a one-celled berry, in which all seeds are contained together.

Cacti are found in many shapes and sizes. Some may grow very large and tall, others take on bush-like dimensions. There are many which remain comparatively miniature throughout the whole span of their lives. Probably by far the greater number are globular in shape and the majority never gain large proportions. On the other hand, columnar species are rarely small in maturity. Many have flat, pad-like branches, as is principally applicable to members of the *Opuntia*. Many genera have leaf-like stems and branches, almost strap-shaped, mainly occurring in the epiphytic genera of *Epiphyllum* and *Rhipsalis*. Just a few species develop real leaves, almost giving the impression of a climbing rose; others have 'pseudo-leaves' which appear on young growth but gradually dry and fall as the branch matures. Most cacti have spines, frequently long and fierce, but many are, or appear to be, entirely spineless.

SUCCULENTS

Following all this, what of the other succulents? These include a host of plants within a great number of genera scattered in many plant families. To give a brief summary of their characteristics would be impossible, but the main groups are dealt with here, these probably being among the most important.

LILIACEAE
Liliaceae (incorporating Asphodelaceae and Hyacinthaceae), groups of the vast lily family, have an outstanding representation, invariably with their leaves in the form of a rosette. They are contained to a large extent in the genera *Aloe*, *Haworthia* and *Gasteria*, most of which are excellent subjects for the beginner. *Aloe* vary tremendously in size and requirements. Leaves can be slender or thick, long or short, fleshy, smooth or rough, warted, often with marginal teeth, and a few are grass-like. In stature they range from the miniature of 5 cm (2 in) or so in diameter to almost giant trees, several metres in height. The long, attractive, lily-like flower spike and numerous flowers are readily forthcoming if the correct growing conditions are provided.

Those within the genus *Haworthia* are mostly stemless, the leaves being mainly fleshy and soft. Just a few have hard leaves armed with hard pointed tubercles, sometimes with minute marginal teeth. Some have the peculiarity of possessing 'windows' at the tips of the leaves, part of the survival kit provided by nature for certain plants which 'draw' themselves into the ground in the harsher, drier times of the year and survive because of the light that penetrates into the plant through the 'window'.

The *Gasteria* genus can easily be mistaken for *Aloe*, but the flowers of the former are distinctive. Several flowers appear on each elongated spike, each flower having a swollen section at the lower part of the flower tube. Flowers are semi-pendant; the upper part is generally greenish, the swollen part more or less reddish. Leaves are a major characteristic of the genus, being somewhat tongue-shaped, generally distichous, that is, developing in two opposite rows, and frequently spirally twisted. They are either smooth and glossy or roughened with few or many raised spots and tubercles; with only few exceptions they are marked beautifully in dark green and greyish variegations and marblings. All species develop plantlets around the base.

MESEMBRYANTHEMACEAE

The Mesembryanthemaceae family (incorporating Aizoaceae) comprises the greatest number of species within the world of 'other succulents'. They are found in numerous forms; many are the so-called 'mimicry' plants, giving the appearance of pebbles or stones, a peculiarity giving rise to the common name of living stones. Several form thick-leaved clusters of dense habit, many are bush-like, others are sprawling, clambering, trailing plants, but all have fleshy 'leaves and bear the typical daisy-like flower in many hues and colours. The seed pod is a characteristic of consequence! When the capsule is fully ripened and when the morning dews descend, it opens into an attractive star-like shape, exposing the minute seeds and allowing them to disperse.

ASCLEPIADACEAE

Another important genus is *Stapelia* contained within the family Asclepiadaceae. This and several other genera of similar shape and habit have proved a most popular and fascinating group. The flowers of *Stapelia* are mostly large and exotic, many have a somewhat obnoxious smell, notwithstanding the well-defined and beautiful appearance of the flower, and this has resulted in their common name carrion plant; in fairness to the genus, there are those which are sweetly scented! In appearance they are three, four, five or more angled, sometimes smooth and glossy, whilst many have a soft velvety surface. Nearly all are of clustering habit, and, with but few exceptions, comparatively dwarf in growth. *Hoya* and *Ceropegia* are two of the climbing or clambering succulents included within this family. They are noted for their unusual flowers, valued as ornamentals for the home and greenhouse. The majority of this family has similar shaped seed pods, these being in the form of a somewhat elongated horn, which, when fully ripened, releases its numerous flattish brown or black seeds attached to parachutes.

EUPHORBIACEAE

Euphorbiaceae are yet another very complex group with characteristics changing from one species to another, or at least, from one group to another. There are definitely many within this vast family which appear very similar to those of some other genus. Many species have prickles, and this often gives rise to confusion between plants of *Euphorbia* and those of some of the cacti species. All have latex, a white milky sap contained within every section of the plant – stem, leaf, root . . . everything. It is wise to remember that this sap can be injurious and painful if it comes into contact with the eyes or mouth, or cuts. Many species of the genus *Euphorbia* grow into large trees, frequently with hard angled branches armed with numerous sharp tubercles. Others are bush-like, sometimes with, sometimes without, leaves. By far the greatest numbers are low growing, developing many peculiar shapes and sizes, so much so that a comprehensive summing-up is impossible, so many have such individual characteristics. This huge Spurge family is known and found throughout the world, but undoubtedly the African succulent species provide the greatest interest. The singular nature of the flower is the principal feature. This is termed a 'cyathium', a small flowering involucre or 'cup' in which the minute flowers are clustered close together. Some species have either totally male or totally female cyathia, and these are often on entirely different plants within the species. In other words, there are literally male and female plants, and seed is likely to be produced only if the two are growing in close proximity, thus making pollination possible.

CRASSULACEAE

The large and diverse family of Crassulaceae includes a predominance of succulents; this is exemplified by the fleshiness of their leaves, stems or root systems. Several genera develop a rosette growth of leaves, and this is especially apparent with *Echeveria, Aeonium, Sempervivum*, the well-known house-leek group, and perhaps, to a lesser degree, with *Crassula* and *Sedum*, many of the latter being better known as stonecrop. Species of *Crassula* and *Sedum* have many guises, particularly the South African Crassulas, where, probably, there are more diversified plant forms than in most other genera of succulents. In habit they vary tremendously, due, no doubt, to their natural habitat conditions. Many are from moist, shady areas; others are native of extreme arid regions. Those from the drier parts are certainly the more fascinating; very often their leaves are clustered closely together so as to form a miniature column or pyramid, the closeness of the leaf structure enabling the plants to withstand periods of drought. Flowers are small, but borne in clusters, and in many instances the flowers are densely set together, resembling a shaving-brush. Very few species are difficult in cultivation, and for this reason can be recommended to the beginner. Another genus of consequence is *Kalanchoe*, several of which have become quite popular houseplants. The

The twisted spines of *Astrophytum capricorne* are a distinctive feature, isolating it from the other attractive species within the genus.

The waxy foliage of *Crassula rosularis* together with the sometimes fasciated flower spike gives it considerable eye-appeal.

essential characteristic is the flower which is decidedly tubular, the four petals being united except at the tips where they separate and recurve. Those which were originally segregated under *Bryophyllum* have the peculiarity of producing numerous plantlets along the margins of the leaves which quickly fall to the ground and grow into substantial plants. All flowers are fairly large or colourful, those of *Bryophyllum* being of pendent habit and perhaps less attractive, whilst other of *Kalanchoe* are erect and frequently borne in clusters with vivid colourings.

AGAVACEAE

One other main family should be mentioned, the Agavaceae. This again is a large family, many species of which are very adaptable to inclement climates, even to the more privileged parts of Britain, where they are used as garden plants. Most species of the *Agave* genus are large-growing, rosette-shaped, and only a few can be satisfactorily contained within the scope of an amateur's greenhouse, at least as mature plants. The leaves are very thick and hard, each with a most pronounced spiny tip and often having the leaf margins armed with thick, hooked teeth. The *Agave* and *Aloe* genera are sometimes confused. The Aloes have an open centre to the rosette, whilst the leaves of *Agave* unfold. The centre of the rosette consists of a thickened 'cone' of yet unopened leaves. As they unfold it will be seen that with most species the opening leaf is indelibly marked on the upper suface by the impression of the back of the leaf next to open. All species require full sun which is an absolute essential to their well-being and development. Flowers occur only on mature plants. Maturity may sometimes be a matter of only a few years, but more often, considerably longer. One of the more common species, *Agave americana*, is referred to as the century plant, due to the fallacy that it only flowers after 100 years, although it is likely 30 to 40 years or more will pass before the giant flower spike appears. Plants die shortly after they flower but leave behind many offsets or plantlets borne from the stolons. Some species form bulbil–like plantlets on the flowering spike which eventually fall and establish as new plants.

There are many other families of succulents of interest, many of which make suitable plants with which to commence a collection. Details and particular characteristics of these will be described later when specific species are described.

CHAPTER 3

GENERAL CULTURE

Certain aspects of culture apply equally whether plants are to be grown as houseplants or in greenhouses.

The composition of the soil is probably the most important feature, but even having the soil right is not necessarily sufficient for successful growing unless all the plants' requirements are provided for. The varieties of compost are possibly the most controversial subject in horticulture. Many branded composts are available from garden shops, garden centres and the like, and there is little doubt that these can be useful as a growing medium. Nevertheless, it is wise to determine the formula and for what purpose it is recommended, and this should be stated on the container. The John Innes composts are excellent, especially if manufactured strictly according to the formula. Likewise, many of the soilless composts available have their advantages. Since the cactus 'cult' has taken hold upon the imagination of the public, brands of 'cactus compost' are offered which provide an easy way for the beginner to select a suitable growing medium for his plants. However, whichever is selected, make absolutely sure that the mixture is really porous – a factor of paramount importance.

All cacti and succulents must be provided with a fool-proof drainage system. Waterlogging can prove disastrous, and the best way to avoid this is to ensure the inclusion of 30% sharp washed sand, grit or fine gravel in the compost. Some branded mixtures do include some sand, whilst soilless composts often have none whatsoever. To overcome this deficiency it is only a matter of adding it yourself, but be certain to use washed material, free from impurities. If you marginally exceed 30%, no harm will ensue, but do not overdo it! If cactus composts are purchased, again be assured that ample grit or sand is included.

It is not difficult to mix your own compost, and sometimes the do-it-yourself method is more satisfactory. If a good garden loam is available, then try the following:

$\frac{1}{3}$ part good, well sterilized loam
$\frac{1}{3}$ part good, thoroughly screened, decomposed leafmould
$\frac{1}{3}$ part good, washed sharp sand, grit or fine gravel
plus a sprinkling of slow-release fertilizer.
(Parts should be measured by volume)

The variation in leaf shape and colour has prompted many to specialize in *Echeveria* species.

Pure loam is not necessarily easy to obtain, due, to a large degree, to the use of so many different herbicides, insecticides, etc., a build-up of which is quite likely to contaminate the soil. When the soil is to be used for pot culture, it is all the more important to take every care. Therefore, if there is any doubt, try peat as an alternative, and add the other two parts as suggested above.

Fertilizing is something which can never be neglected – it prevents starvation. If a plant looks sad or off-colour, don't add fertilizer until you are aware of the reason for its appearance. Firstly determine the cause by examining the root structure, which is frequently the problem. It may be that repotting is necessary, all the goodness in the soil having been used up. Fertilizing in such cases would do more harm than good. It is far better to trim the ill-affected roots, repot into a good soil, allow to establish and become obviously healthy with new growth appearing, before feeding.

Try to purchase an all-sufficient product. Branded fertilizers should state the formula. Nitrogen and potash are, of course, necessary for success, but endeavour to obtain one which contains the essential trace elements of iron, magnesium, copper, boron, manganese and molybdenum, which all have an important role to play in producing the quality plant required.

One other fact to remember concerning peat-based composts, which applies to all soilless products, is that the manufacturers include fertilizers, but the tendency is for these to become rapidly exhausted, either by the demand of the plant, or from seepage when excess moisture drains away. It is probable that regular fertilizing is even more necessary in such circumstances.

One last important rule: only apply fertilizer when plants are in growth, never when dormant!

GREENHOUSE CULTIVATION

It is as well to remember that we are using unnatural methods in growing; nature never ordained that plants should grow under glass, or for that matter, in pots! However, the enthusiastic plantsman generally tries to introduce exotics into his world of 'growing things', and we have to adopt certain measures to do so. The greenhouse is as good a sanctuary as any, especially for succulents, since a well-built structure makes possible the controlled conditions necessary to guarantee satisfactory growth.

Make certain the greenhouse is *leak-proof*. Nothing damages succulent plants more than drip. So often the likelihood of moisture penetrating is at a time of year when plants must be kept completely dry and permitted to go dormant. Equally dangerous are draughts, but they should be fairly simple to deal with. *Ventilation* is yet another aspect to consider; plants rarely tolerate a stuffy atmosphere, but they do not want too much at the wrong time. Ventilation is necessary to stimulate growth and prevent stagnation. Mechanical devices are available to produce a perfect ventilating system, and these are to be recommended. When there is no-one at hand to tend the greenhouse, it is satisfying to have equipment which opens and closes the ventilators as required; these being mainly temperature-controlled.

Another essential chore – keep the glass clean. Whilst it is not necessarily important to have sun, in fact too much could prove harmful as it may become magnified through the glass and cause scorch, *good light* must be provided.

Mention has been made of the scorching of plants, and this can frequently happen far too easily with cacti and succulents. In the heat of a brilliant summer, when there are long periods or sunshine, a degree of *shading* can prove invaluable. Various forms of materials can be purchased, either in the form of blinds or an external shading spray. In the latter case, remove it once the need has gone.

The necessity of providing suitable *heating*, when weather conditions demand, is another item of importance. Whatever equipment is installed, make certain the apparatus is fume-proof. If fumes build up in a green-house, extensive damage will result, so seek the best advice possible when selecting the heating equpment. With regard to temperatures, most species will be perfectly content during the dormant season if 7–10°C (45–50°F) is maintained – a period of the year which more or less co-incides with the winter months of the northern hemisphere. During dormancy, that is from late autumn to early spring, keep your plants completely dry, and only commence watering when the weather pattern appears to have improved and is likely to remain constant.

After the resting season, *watering* becomes a matter of great care. It might be wise to mention types of pots at this stage. Which to use, either clay or plastic, is purely a matter of choice and opinion, and whatever has been given in the way of advice applies equally, whatever the pot. It must be stressed, however, that clay pots dry out far quicker than plastic ones and invariably the latter require less frequent attention in this respect than clay pots.

Watering is an all-important aspect for successful culture. When to water? If in doubt – don't! It is far better to be cautious than reckless, for watering at the wrong time, or over-watering, can be deemed exceed-ingly harmful to all such plants. After the rest season, apply water very carefully at first, then increase as weather conditions improve and pots dry out quicker. When this period arrives, water *well*; wait until the pots dry out, then water again thoroughly. This process can be repeated throughout the growing and flowering season. Never leave pots standing in water as this prevents good drainage. Likewise, little 'spoonfuls' each day are just as bad, or worse; plants *must* use their nourishment, otherwise they get their own peculiar form of 'indigestion' as they have no natural resistance to this. The tendency would then be for rot to set in, and if incorrect watering is the reason, they rot from the roots up!

It is not essential to give water from the base; do so, if you wish, but when the plants have taken up sufficient water, then allow the pots to drain and any surplus moisture to seep away. Overhead watering is very satisfactory, and, in fact, helps to keep plants looking clean. As long as the soil is porous and excess water is not permitted to remain, there is a great deal to say in favour of overhead spraying. One warning, however: never water overhead during the heat of the day, the more so when the sun is full on the greenhouse! Better to undertake this task well before the sun reaches its zenith, so enabling any moisture remaining on the plants to gradually disperse as the temperature rises. Alternatively, late after-noon or early evening watering can be recommended.

As to watering or not watering, it is purely a matter of emulating the plants' natural conditions as sensibly as possible. In habitat there are

The roots spread naturally

crocking

Fig. 1 When potting a cactus ensure that there is sufficient room to allow the roots to spread naturally and that the pot is well crocked.

periods of drought and seasonal rainstorms, and between these two extremes, plants really dry out. Remember also, many arid areas are not without their morning dews, a phenomenon which contributes to the well-being of the plants in general!

Great care should be exercised in *potting* (Fig. 1). This can be done at almost any period of the year, except when the plant is in bud or flower; disturbance at this time is very likely to stop flowering for the season. The best months to choose are those towards the end of the dormant season and before the plants begin to develop new roots or growth.

It is imperative to use a container of suitable size to contain the plant. Over-potting or under-potting is equally to be deplored – nothing looks worse than a plant obviously too small or too large for its pot! Apart from the porous compost, the process of potting should encourage porosity. Good crocking is essential, not just a matter of covering the hole at the bottom. It is necessary to place crocking in the base of the pot to a depth of 1–2 cm ($\frac{1}{2}$–$\frac{3}{4}$ in) or more, dependent upon the size and depth of the container. Either broken pieces of pot or sharp 1–2 cm ($\frac{1}{2}$–$\frac{3}{4}$ in) gravel are very suitable; also, add charcoal chippings to combat any souring of the soil.

In the process of planting, make sure the roots are spread apart, not crushed together, and also make certain that any broken or damaged roots are cleanly severed. Then place sufficient soil to cover the crocking, hold the plant in position with the roots hanging naturally, gently add soil to within 1 cm ($\frac{1}{2}$ in) of the top of the pot, tapping the pot to encourage the soil to settle. Finally firm the surface with thumb and fingers. The soil mixture should be *just* moist, not dry; and allow a few days to pass before watering.

CULTIVATION AS HOUSEPLANTS

Much that has been said already applies equally well when the emphasis is solely on using plants for home decoration. Whilst most species will adapt themselves to the somewhat restricted environment of the house, there are many which appear to be just as content or even more so than when kept in a greenhouse. Hence the important thing is to learn which plants are best suited. It is, of course, very true that for years many species have tended to be grown just for the home such as sansevierias, hoyas, Christmas cacti and many others. There is no doubt that with careful selection, a great number of these exotics can prove beautiful acquisitions.

Many of the cacti whose ancestry was the jungle, make wonderful subjects for home culture. The Christmas and Easter cacti are two of the finest examples. *Epiphyllum* species, likewise, are ideally suited and perhaps even more so, the cultivars; they are many and beautiful. Most of the species of this genus are night-flowering, and heavily scented, with large exotic blooms, but even more popular are the host of colourful cultivars now available in shades of pink, red, orange, purple, yellow, cream and white; these are day-flowering with blooms from 5 cm (2 in) to 30 cm (12 in) in diameter. Many specialist nurseries offer extensive lists of these plants; a very few outstanding varieties are as follows:

'Alba Superba'	large white, scented, day-flowering
'Amber Queen'	rich, deep orange
'Chauncey'	multi-coloured, red, orange, purple
'Deutsche Kaiserin'	smallish flower, shades of rose and pink

'Fortuna'	funnel-shaped flower, scented, pink
'Guatemala'	very deep red and purple, large flower
'Kinchinjunga'	peculiar but attractive shaped flower, cream-white
'King Midas'	very large golden yellow with deeper stripe
'Queen Anne'	yellow with frilled edges to petals, scented
'Royal Token'	deep orange-red, large flower
'Scarletina'	somewhat small reddish flower
'Thalia'	red, purple and magenta, large flower
'Zoe'	begonia pink, large, choice flower

These are representatives of many, and without exception will produce a continuity of flowers from mid-spring to mid-summer. Before leaving this selection, it would be improper not to refer to 'Ackermannii' – a beautiful, floriferous cultivar with bright red flowers and triangular stems – one which has graced the homes of so many for nearly a century.

The temptation is to enlarge on the outstanding plants suitable for the home, but these will be mentioned in detail later in the book.

However, now to their culture. If they are to be pot grown, much the same techniques will apply as those for greenhouse culture. Remember, however, that plants such as those mentioned have a background which has its origin in forest country where a richer compost can be provided, more humus and less soil. If totally decomposed cow manure can be obtained, this would prove the most superior fertilizer of all. However, drainage, watering, fertilizing, etc. requirements do not vary, but be careful not to place plants in a dull corner. Give them light, but not where full sun is shining on them for long periods. With epiphyllums it can prove beneficial to stand the pots out-of-doors after flowering is over, preferably under the shade of a tree, where they can be watered readily and generally cared for. If brought back indoors in early autumn, before the frosts set in, they will quickly begin, from early winter onwards, to show flower buds, and will prove to be more healthy and vigorous, and possibly with more flowers developing.

In general, there are relatively few well-known cacti and succulents which fail to succeed in the home; succulents in particular readily adapt themselves, although the problem with some will be the lack of sunshine and good light, and this could lead to etiolation and no flowers. However, with care, many species can be used, especially for bowl garden planting, and good preparation of the bowl is crucial.

Most such containers have no holes in the base, and therefore careful planning is required. Any bowl less than 10 cm (4 in) deep is better not used as sufficient depth of crocking must be allowed for. So it is a matter of the deeper the better. Crocking should be of suitable depth, certainly not less than 2.5 cm (1 in) when only a 10 cm (4 in) bowl is used. In other words, endeavour to allow for a quarter of the depth of the container to be crocked. Unless this rule is observed, too much water could accumulate and set up root rot. Soil should be just moist when potting. The best way to ascertain whether water is necessary is by use of a hydrometer.

CHAPTER 4

PROPAGATION

The art of propagation is not difficult and there are different methods which can be adopted; each with due care, can offer excellent results.

SEED PROPAGATION

This system has many advantages, and whilst perhaps slower, it can prove to be a very fascinating and rewarding method. It is, of course, infinitely cheaper to rear plants in this way as much seed can be purchased for the price of one plant! Then again, if you are assured that the seed comes from plants true to type, the resulting seedling will not prove to be a 'query case'; you immediately have authentic naming, and that to any collector is very satisfying. Plants grown from seed readily adapt to their environment right from the beginning when germination takes place, and that, in itself, is important; after all, what can prove more satisfying than to look at a plant in later years, when it is thoroughly matured in growth, with the realization it is of your own raising!

Most seeds of cacti and succulents are viable for a long period, but there are numerous exceptions. It is the best policy to make certain that your purchase is a new season's crop, and if such is the case, very good germination will result. Mixed seed can be obtained quite easily from garden sundriesmen; the product may result in quite a variety of different species and then you might be faced with the difficulty of ascertaining the correct nomenclature. One other difficulty might arise also, the fact that mixed seeds are not only of different species, but also differ in size and in the period of germination. Whilst some will germinate in a matter of days, others can remain weeks or even months before germinating, so care must be taken to avoid the temptation of presuming 'nothing will come', and discard the compost from the container. Furthermore, seeing that larger seeds require covering to about the depth of the diameter of the seeds, problems might occur with the finer or dust-like seed which needs only to be sown finely over the surface of the compost and watered in. Therefore, it would appear far better to know what you are sowing; in other words, purchase named species, then you can sow accordingly, and obtain far better and more gratifying results.

There are many brands of seed composts on the market, and most of these can be of use when sowing cactus seeds. When preparing the container it is important to cover the base with really porous compost, as drainage is a particular requirement. It is also wise to add charcoal chippings to this basal covering so as to help prevent souring of the soil mixture. Then fill the container with the seed compost to within approx. 1 cm ($\frac{1}{2}$ in) of the rim, firm the compost well to produce a completely level surface so that when watering is done, no excess moisture gathers into one space. As suggested above, the seeds can be of various sizes and shapes; the dust-like ones can be sprinkled evenly over the surface and carefully watered in, trying not to allow the seeds to become affixed to each other. Other seeds of larger dimensions should be covered very lightly with compost or, even better, fine sharp sand, to a depth about equal to the diameter of the seeds being sown. Be careful not to bury the seeds deeply as this retards or prevents germination. Many species will begin to germinate quickly if placed in a somewhat humid atmosphere of about 20°C (70°F). Containers should be in a very shaded area throughout the germination period, then gradually given more light and ventilation as the little seedlings begin to develop, but NOT full sun. To summarize:

Preparation of the container is very important.
Level surface to the soil is equally essential.
Seeds are covered to a depth of the diameter of the seeds.
Dust seed can be sprinkled evenly over the surface and lightly watered in; containers with larger seeds are best placed in a tray or bowl of tepid water to allow the whole compost to be thoroughly moistened.
Containers are placed in shady position at correct temperature. These can be covered with glass or paper which will help provide the shade and humidity, but beware of too much of the latter, in other words if moisture gathers on the inside of the glass, wipe it off, as drips from this on to the seeds can do harm.
When seedlings appear, begin to give more light and ventilation.

The best time to sow is early in the year – mid-winter to early spring is ideal – and this means a great responsibility to maintain the temperature at the correct level. By sowing at this time, it enables the seedlings to be grown on for a period of at least nine months without resting, and it can prove amazing how much growth is made in this period. If facilities permit, it is wise to continue this growth throughout the following winter and summer, by which time a fairly well-developed plant will result.

Of all the problems with seedlings, the worst is, undoubtedly, damping-off; this can be very dangerous. Therefore it is better to provide against it before it occurs. There are several compounds, the qualities of which have

Echinocactus grusonii is rightfully called the golden-barrel cactus. The golden spines are prominently in evidence from seedling stage to full maturity.

been well tested and proven satisfactory against this disease: Cheshunt compound, captan or zineb – these and others are equally good. Mix with water, according to instructions on the package, and lightly spray the seedlings at their first watering after germination. Prevention is better than cure!

When to prick out seedlings? Do not be too hasty; if the seedlings are not too close together they can remain in the container for many months without coming to harm. Even if overcrowded they will not necessarily suffer being left for a long period. The general guide-line, however, is to wait until they are large enough to handle and have taken on the semb-lance of the parent plant; with cacti, it is best to wait until the minute spines appear. The best time to prick out is early spring – care should be taken to maintain a temperature conducive to continuing growth.

CUTTINGS

Cuttings (vegetative propagation) is another interesting method to try. Many cacti and succulents develop 'offsets' (Fig. 2); these frequently have

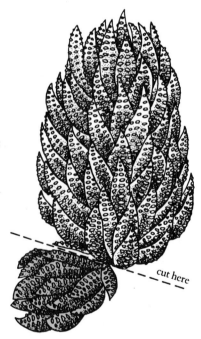

Fig. 2 Vegetative propagation. Many cacti and succulents develop 'offsets'; these frequently have roots at an early stage and can be carefully removed from the parent and potted on in the normal way.

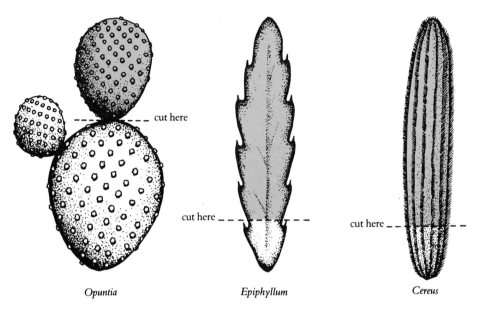

Opuntia   Epiphyllum   Cereus

Fig. 3 Some examples of cacti cuttings, showing where the cut should be made.

roots at an early stage and therefore can be removed carefully and potted on in the normal way. Many species of cacti are readily propagated by literally severing a section from the parent plant, allowing it to callus for several days and setting the cutting in a very sandy compost, with, preferably, under-heat. The cuttings should be away from full sun and kept reasonably dry; rooting often commences within a week or so with many species, and once roots are established, they may be potted as normal plants.

Many of the 'other succulents' can be propagated by cuttings (Fig 3). Suitable subjects are to be found among the Mesembryanthemaceae, Crassulaceae, Euphorbiaceae, Asclepiadaceae and similar stem-growing groups. To deal separately with each group would cover many pages; suffice it to say that most species can be multiplied by severing the stem, allowing to callus, then planting as with cacti.

Others are able to develop new plants from leaf cuttings: this applies particularly to members of the Crassulaceae (*Echeveria, Sedum, Crassula, Adromischus,* etc.). These should be inserted into a tray of clean and fairly sharp, coarse sand: roots develop very fast, and once these appear and strengthen, they can be potted on without hesitation. Many euphorbias can be propagated by stem cuttings, but more care must be exercised! If it is possible it is better to make the cut where the branch joins the main

stem. Remember also that all euphorbias have milky sap, and the parent plant and cutting commence to 'bleed' directly they are severed. This can best be stopped by placing the cut section in cold water for a few minutes, then allowing to dry and callus and treating as other stem cuttings. The bushy mesembryanthemums root very fast from cuttings and are probably the least problematic in this form of propagation.
The main factors therefore are:

> Always use a sharp, clean knife – remember it *is* an operation!
>
> *Only* mature growth should be used, not new stems, branches, etc. just appearing!
>
> Always allow cuts to callus well before setting.
>
> Compost must be *very* sandy, preferably with charcoal added. Keep fairly dry for cacti, and just moist for succulents.
>
> Under-heat or a total all-round temperature of 20°C (70°F) helps rooting, and good light is not harmful.
>
> *Never* take cuttings in cold or damp weather!

GRAFTING

This is a vogue which has become increasingly popular in more recent years, the more so since seedlings without chlorophyll (coloured red, yellow, etc.) have become popular. Grafting for grafting's sake is to be deplored as many plants develop far better on their own roots, but, of course, there are numerous exceptions. If a species is exceedingly slow growing, temperamental in our climatic conditions, cristated or fasciated, lacking effectiveness because of its somewhat unpredictable growth, or if seedlings without chlorophyll are wanted, then grafting can be of tremendous advantage.

There are a number of very slow growing cacti – possibly the best example is *Blossfeldia* (although this really should be considered a plant for the more advanced collector). A seedling remains almost pin-head size for ages, and whilst grafting of this is far from easy, once grafted, the growth is accelerated beyond belief. However, in a case like this, do not attempt to graft a seedling before it can be handled and 'operated' on without undue difficulty. This applies equally to those plants without chlorophyll. The idea was developed by the Japanese; seedlings of these 'freak' plants which normally died after the cotyledon had withered, were grafted on to suitable stock thus enabling the little seedling to live and grow, and incidentally, flower too!

Epiphyllum cultivar seedlings can be grafted to bring them to flowering maturity faster, but it is not essential once they have reached

An example of the colourful flowers of the genus *Echinocereus*. This varietal form of *Echinocereus fendleri* was discovered near the border of California with Nevada.

Echinopsis species readily cross-pollinate with other species of the genus and also with those of *Lobivia*, resulting in flowers of many varying shades of colour.

this stage to keep them grafted; they may be removed, allowed to callus, then set to allow rooting to take place.

The whole process of grafting consists simply of uniting a stem cutting, such as a seedling, or a cutting from a mature plant (this being termed the 'scion'), to the stem of another growing plant, called the 'stock'. The operation must be a thorough one, and it calls for every care and attention, plus the use of very sharp tools; a blunt knife cannot be used and could mean a useless result from the beginning! Neither cut must be allowed to dry off before the two are affixed, as the principle is literally to unite the two together and form one plant. The best time to undertake this task is in early summer, at a time when plants are in active growth, the main contributor to fusing the two together effectively.

There are different ways of grafting cacti, the system usually varies according to what is being grafted. The commonest method is a *flat graft* Fig (4a), this simply being a straight cut across both the scion and the stock, the two cut surfaces being reasonably compatible, and the edges of the stock being carefully bevelled so that any drying out of the edges does not detach the scion. The two can be held together by rubber bands which should be left for a sufficient period until union of the two is complete. This system is generally adopted for globular species or cristates.

The *cleft graft* Fig. (4b) is more suited to species with thin stems or segments, such as *Schlumbergera, Epiphyllum* and certain *Rhipsalis*. The procedure is to make a 'V' shaped cut in the stock, and the scion is cut to a similar shape so that they fit perfectly together without undue pressure. Insert the scion, fasten the two together with a fine cactus spine and then bind around with raffia or a rubber band so as to keep the cut areas on both stock and scion firmly held together. Failure to do this may result in shrinkage and possibly the failure of the union. It may take a few weeks before the binding and spine can be removed; do not be too impatient, for the essential thing is that the cell tissues of both are totally fused as one.

Another somewhat less used method is the *side graft* (Fig 4c). This is simply a matter of cutting the scion and stock diagonally, actually providing a larger area of contact. Place the two cut areas together, fix with a sharp cactus spine, then bind carefully but firmly as with the cleft graft method. It is also recommended that a slender cane should be used to support the graft, both stock and scion, during fusion.

Almost any species of cactus can be grafted, but it is most important that the best stock is selected for the particular operation. Many of the tall growing species make excellent stock, such as *Echinopsis spachianus, Echinopsis pachanoi* (better known as *Trichocereus*), *Selenicereus grandiflorus,*

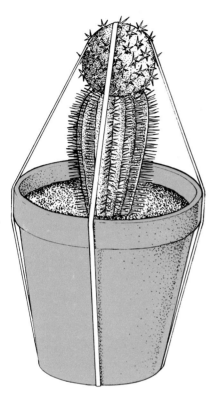

Fig. 4 Types of grafts.

Flat graft (left). Support the scion and the stock by means of rubber bands, which will hold them firmly together until union is accomplished.

Cleft graft (below left)
A Cut a 'V' shape in the stock.
B Similarly shape the scion.
C Insert and fix the two with spine and raffia.

Side graft (below right).
D Give support to both scion and stock with cane and bind each together, and each separately to the supporting cane.

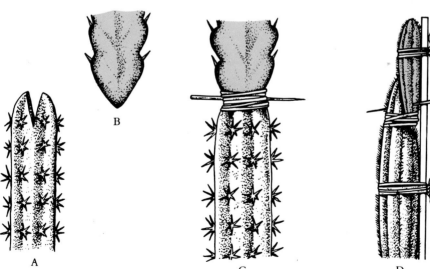

A

B

C

D

Hylocereus spp. and many more, but it is always necessary to try and select the right one. It will be found that *Selenicereus* is to be preferred to any other when it comes to cleft grafting of *Schlumbergera* and the like. The stocky younger growths of *Echinopsis pachanoi* and *Echinopsis spachianus* are well suited for most of the more globular types, whether they be young growths cut from mature plants or young seedlings. It invariably applies that the seedlings and offsets of species without chlorophyll (the red, yellow or whitish coloured plants) are grafted to *Hylocereus* which certainly speeds up the growth and vitality of the scion, but unfortunately it is not always the easiest stock to maintain as it requires a slightly

Fig. 5 *Grafting a succulent.*
A The scion (say, *Tavaresia*).
B The stock (*Stapelia*).
C Supporting cane.
D Plastic 'platform' with hole inserted to slip over top of cane.
E Small weight (stone) to give light pressure to help hold scion and stock together.

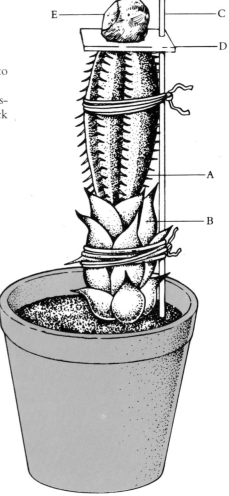

higher temperature, plus more moisture, and unless this is forthcoming the stock tends either to dehydrate or rot. It would therefore appear better to use *Echinopsis spachianus* or even *Myrillocactus geometrizens,* which, generally speaking, are sounder stock, even if, the scion is slightly slower in its growth.

Many of the 'other succulents' can be grafted if suitable care is taken. Certain of the species within the family Asclepiadaceae are exceedingly difficult on their own roots in cultivation; *Hoodia* and *Tavaresia* are just two genera of many which present problems, even to the experienced collector. Some species of the same family are nevertheless reasonably easy to grow, and are certainly to be included among those suited to beginners. Several species, in particular *Orbea (Stapelia) variegata,* are relatively hardy to normal greenhouse conditions, and as such, provide very convenient grafting stock for the more difficult species. In all such cases, it is a matter of using the *flat graft* technique, making sure that the two cut surfaces are of equal size, binding them to a slender cane for support and holding the two together as shown in Fig 5 until the union is assured. So many more species of other families can be similarly treated – *Euphorbia* and *Kalanchoe* are typical – but remember, that it is policy to *only* graft when necessary, for no plant really looks better than when it is growing naturally on its own roots.

One word of warning! If you have not undertaken this sort of propagation before, then start with the commoner plants; do not choose the choicest! Try to master the subject before starting on the more rare and uncommon material. It is also as well to remember the purpose for which you are grafting: if there is no need for it, do not do it, as grafts are mostly made for accelerating growth or dealing with the more temperamental species, *not* just to create a grafted specimen, and grafts are not necessarily permanent.

CHAPTER 5

PESTS AND DISEASES

Unfortunately succulent plants are not immune to insect infestation and disease, and, in fact, unless particular care is observed, they easily fall prey to pests and other problems. However, with due attention, it is no great chore to maintain a healthy and vigorous collection.

Many pests are liable to cause damage to both cacti and succulents, but fortunately we live in days when numerous different insecticides are available, many of which are ideally suited to our plants and will undoubtedly help towards maintaining a pest-free collection. Indirectly, ants are one of the biggest nuisances, and whilst they themselves do not directly damage the plant, they are one of the main 'distributors' of some of the pests which create most problems, such as mealy bug, greenfly and the like. It would therefore seem wise to try and eradicate ants from the greenhouse: they never serve any useful purpose and are better destroyed.

Diseases, on the other hand, are most frequently due to incorrect treatment or negligence; under-watering and over-watering are equally dangerous and can cause endless difficulties with the root systems, setting up rot which spreads to the whole plant structure. Bruising is yet another cause of disease; this is often due to mishandling, affecting the body of the plant firstly, but rapidly involving the roots as well. So it must be obvious that many things can be avoided if care is taken.

Whilst there are antidotes to the majority of problems, it certainly behoves every collector to ensure that it is the exception, not the rule, to have pests and disease; many preventatives can be purchased to keep these enemies at bay. Deal with the situation before it arrives! With pests, in particular, systemic insecticides are available which will guarantee healthy and insect-free plants all the time.

However, here are a few suggestions to deal with the situation if it arises, and a list of some of the common pests and problems.

PESTS

Mealy bug This is one of the most pernicious of pests and unless completely eradicated it can spoil both the appearance of the plant, and the plant itself. This is the creature which was formerly used to manufacture cochineal and thousands of them were bred for this purpose, generally on species of *Opuntia*. It can appear in various guises, as there are several species, but the commonest one is that which attacks cacti, especially, it would seem, in cultivation. They have the appearance of a small woodlouse, whitish or greyish, and covered with a white, wax-like substance. The eggs are found covered by white tufts, and scientists tell us this pest lays about 600 eggs each time; this appears to occur two or three times each year, so this is definitely a pest to get rid of completely, or results could be disastrous. At the first appearance it is advisable to use one part nicotine to three parts methylated spirit, applying with a small paint brush directly to the insect or the nest. As a control, use a systemic insecticide which is taken up by plant, and anything that tries to feed on it dies. Alternatively, use diluted malathion as prescribed on the bottle.

Root mealy bug This is a smaller insect than the typical mealy bug, and it sucks moisture from the roots, causing the plant to lose its vitality and generally look sick. This pest is often present when there is any infestation of ants, especially if the plant is in a pot; the ants centre around and in the pot and seem to encourage the creatures. There are several ways of dealing with the situation. If the plant is de-potted it will be found that the roots are covered with a fine mealy substance, almost powdery; this can be removed by gently washing with tepid water. Then dip the roots in a malathion solution and re-pot. Alternatively, the pot can be immersed in warm water to which has been added either nicotine or malathion (about a small level teaspoonful to 1 litre (1.7pt) of water), left for about 30 minutes, and then allowed to drain thoroughly. The more modern system is the use of systemic insecticides, and there are several; any of these watered into the soil will provide a cure or preventive, whichever is called for.

Scale insects These pests very quickly disfigure the plant unless immediate attention is given. They are minute insects covered by a whitish, shell-like covering, slightly larger than a pinhead, resembling a limpet. The insect lays its eggs under the covering of the shell; when these are hatched they crawl around seeking a suitable feeding area where they live by sucking the sap; once this has been found, they become immobile and in due course form their own shell. In the early stages they can almost be wiped away, but the shell gradually hardens and it becomes necessary to spray with, preferably, an oil-based insecticide such as Volck. There should be no problem in purchasing sprays which deal promptly and effectively with the pest; as a preventive, a systemic insecticide containing malathion will help to keep this pest away indefinitely.

White fly and greenfly Both these insects are equally destructive, and their presence is encouraged by ants. White fly, in particular, are very persistent, tending to attack certain succulents, such as *Euphorbia* species, as well as many other cacti and succulents. Once again, prevention is better than cure; use systemics periodically when watering and this will help to keep plants immune. If the pests have taken hold, then HCH 'smokes' in the greenhouse will help to kill white fly. Alternatively, sprays containing pyrethrum or bioresmethrin will deal with the situation. Greenfly are much simpler to destroy, and many sprays other than those mentioned for white fly are offered by garden sundriesmen.

Red spider mite This is a pest which appears to attack plants which are kept too dry for too long in warm weather. They develop in colonies of minute, orange-red creatures, surrounded by very fine webs. Individually the insect is hardly discernible to the naked eye, but failure to deal with the situation means disfigurement of the plant. The insects suck the sap, and generally the cacti or the leaves of the succulents turn brown, and remain so! To discourage the introduction of red spider mite, provide good ventilation; furthermore they dislike a humid atmosphere, so if a combination of these factors can be produced, the likelihood of trouble is lessened. The best answer to cure the problem is systemics; in fact there is no doubt that most problems can be avoided if systemic insecticides are applied regularly when watering.

Sciarid fly This is often referred to as the mushroom fly; a minute, greyish fly which lays its eggs in the soil. These hatch into little white grubs which eat the roots of both seedlings and mature plants. They usually occur with peat-based composts or in composts where humus has been included which was not thoroughly decomposed prior to mixing. Effective control is obtained by watering the plants with a spray-strength malathion liquid.

Nematodes These are known as eelworms, and they attack the root systems of plants, causing swellings or 'galls' to develop; these contain numerous tiny worms, each too small to see. If left unattended, they rapidly ruin the plants which turn yellowish and cease to grow. Drastic action is essential, even to the removing of all the roots and parts of the stem until there is no trace of discoloration left by the infestation. Dust the cut areas with sulphur powder, allow to callus, and then re-pot, keeping reasonably dry until re-rooted. There are chemical treatments available, and some of these will advise protective clothing. However, in Britain and other northern hemisphere countries where cold winters are experienced, the problem is less likely to arise.

Echinopsis smrzianus is typical of the taller growing plants originally included in the genus *Trichocereus*. Flowers are night-flowering and slightly scented.

Other pests could be mentioned: *slugs and snails*, for which pellets are prescribed for rapid effect. *Woodlice*, which can prove destructive to seedlings, can be controlled with HCH dust. *Ants* can be readily dealt with as there are many products available for this purpose; failure to deal with the situation can cause other indirect difficulties.

DISEASES

If a plant is kept healthy, and regular attention is given to its essential requirements, disease is very unlikely to occur. However, certain unpleasant diseases can arise, and when visible, should have urgent attention.

Damping-off This is generally associated with seedlings, and the remedy has been suggested in an earlier chapter. However, to reiterate, use a good fungicide such as Cheshunt compound, captan or zineb; these and others will have satisfying results.

Black rot This is most frequent with certain species of the Asclepiadaceae family, and a few of the epiphytic cacti. The blackening of the stem usually occurs just below the soil level, and often the damage is done before we are aware of it. It is thought to be caused by infection entering the stem through a break in the skin tissues. It is also thought to be associated with too high a nitrogen content in the soil. The remedy is to remove the affected parts by cutting away with a sharp knife, dusting with sulphur powder, allowing to callus and then setting for re-rooting. Prevention lies with copper-based fungicides being applied periodically.

Other less problematic diseases may occur if due care is not given to your plants regularly. *Decay* can happen if plants are over-watered, bruised or exposed to extreme cold or drip. *Scorch* can occur if attention is not paid to *when* to water—never in full sun! *Rust* can occur if water is retained too long on the exposed body of the plant. It is all a matter of keeping careful watch—a plant soon shows when it is in need of special treatment.

WARNING

Insecticides, fungicides and certain other chemicals used in horticulture are highly poisonous, and extreme care must be taken when handling these things. The dosage must be correct. Often protective clothing is recommended. *Always* wash your hands after using any of these commodities. Store in a safe place, away from children and pets.

PART II
SELECTION OF
EASILY GROWN SPECIES

This record is not intended as a complete survey of all the plants which can be grown readily by the beginner, but rather to emphasize those which are more easily available and should offer relatively few problems in cultivation. Furthermore, preference is given to species which have desirable characteristics, such as shape, foliage attraction and floral appeal, the latter, of course, being the aspect of greatest importance. It must not be presumed that all species within any particular genus are equally suitable for beginners; the chances are that some of the most easy to grow are generically linked with others whose cultivation requires considerable skill. Sufficient details will be given to help identify a species, where it originates, where it is most likely to flourish in cultivation, the essential requirements, and also the plant family to which it belongs.

Acanthocalycium CACTACEAE

This is a comparatively small genus of globular plants from Argentina, having many pronounced ribs and heavily spined. *A. aurantiacum* is from high altitudes, with perhaps fewer spines than others and attractive orange-yellow flowers. *A. violaceum* has a darker green body with very many more spines and ribs with rich, lilac-purple flowers. These are not necessarily common plants, but can be purchased from most specialist nurseries and will prove to be something really different. A light position in the greenhouse is preferred and flowers develop during late spring and summer. Water must be withheld completely during dormancy and given carefully at all other times.

Adromischus CRASSULACEAE

This is quite a large genus whose attraction is largely centred in the foliage. All species are native to South Africa, from Cape Province across to Transvaal. The flowers are somewhat insignificant, but invariably the leaf shapes and markings more than compensate. *A. cristatus* is a miniature with fleshy leaves, the tips of which form an undulating 'ridge'. *A. festivus* has leaves resembling plover eggs; thick, almost completely egg-shaped, except for the somewhat blunted tips. It never ceases to be dwarf in character, but the development of new leaves eventually provides quite a large cluster. *A. maculatus* is yet another miniature of consequence; the leaves are somewhat flat, almost heart-shaped, and beautifully

The cultivar '*Deutsche Kaiserin*' is one of the very earliest produced and by some thought to be an improved form of *Nopalxochia phyllanthoides*, one of the parents.

marked and mottled reddish-brown. All species must have a sunny aspect to produce the best colouring of the leaves. Whilst watering must be restricted during their rest period, they are nevertheless not too sensitive to moisture in moderation. Flowers appear during the summer months. They are suitable for greenhouse and home culture, and perhaps particularly good for bowl gardens. Soil must be very porous, and again, the emphasis is on a very sunny, bright position.

Aeonium CRASSULACEAE

This large genus of rosette plants includes quite easy subjects for beginners which, with few exceptions, will thrive under normal greenhouse conditions; if given good sunlight, most will flower with bright yellow or whitish blooms during late winter and spring. All are indigenous to the Canary Islands, Madeira and parts of North Africa, and are closely related to the well-known houseleeks, *Sempervivum*. The best known is undoubtedly *A. arboreum* which, if encouraged, can reach to 1 m (3¼ ft) in height. It is a species of erect habit, often branching towards the top, each branch with rosettes of thin, ciliate-edged leaves and flowers in elongated racemes of golden-yellow florets. There are also varietal forms such as *var. atropurpureum* with rich, reddish-purple leaves, and *var. luteovariegatum* with distinctive, yellow-mottled leaf markings. *A. haworthii* is a much smaller-growing plant, bush-like in habit and branching freely. Leaves are dull greyish-green, edged red and the flowers are in loose clusters, creamy-white in colour. *A. tabulaeforme* has a completely flattened rosette to 30 cm (1 ft) diameter. *A. sedifolium* has smaller leaves than the other species, these being quite fleshy and becoming reddened in the sun. The plant is rarely more than about 15 cm (6 in) high and forms dense little bushes. All these plants are for a sunny area of a greenhouse, although, if suitable provision can be made, they will give every satisfaction as houseplants. None is susceptible to rot so watering presents little difficulty, although a drying-off period after flowering is recommended.

Agave AGAVACEAE

This large genus includes a great number of large-growing plants, generally too big in maturity to be housed under glass and certainly not in the home! Their native home is mainly southern parts of USA, Mexico and certain of the West Indian islands. Only few can be considered suitable for normal greenhouse culture, and their main appeal is in the fascinating, regular rosette formation of the leaves. *A. filifera* is a stemless species with dark green leaves with white markings, and numerous fine white threads along the leaf margins. *A. americana* is one of the larger-growing species which is outside the scope of the average greenhouse, but *var. mediopicta alba* is well worth including in the collection, especially as a young plant, because of its distinctive white central stripe along each leaf. *A. victoriae-reginae* is one of the most eye-catching species. If grown properly it forms compact, round rosettes of short, very thick leaves with attractive whitish markings and horn-like margins, each leaf tipped with a dark brown spine. There are others, too, which should be mentioned; *A. stricta* with its slender, needle-like leaves, rounded and very narrow, and *A. utahensis*, a compact, small-growing species with grey-green rosettes, the margins of the leaves being sinuate with pronounced hooked, triangular teeth. A very neat species, *A. shawii*, is from the Baja California – the rosettes are very compact with glossy-green leaves 30–50 cm (12–20 in) long and 12 cm (4½ in) across with a pronounced terminal spine about 4cm (1½ in) long – the margins are toothed and horny. *A. parviflora* has a small rosette of about 15 cm (6 in) diameter – the leaves dark-green marked with whitish lines and a small terminal spine, the margins add an attraction with the whitish, fibrous threads along the upper part of the leaves. From such a small plant comes an inflorescence of over 1 m (3¼ ft) in length. This is from more northerly parts of Mexico. *A. arizonica* is another species with a small rosette – about 40 cm (16 in) diameter – comprised of fairly erect leaves of deep-green which have a terminal spine and small downward-pointing teeth along the margins. From Arizona, USA. All species come from regions where they suffer a long drought season, so it is imperative that moisture is withheld from, say, late autumn to early spring. A bright position is beneficial, but not necessarily full sun; in fact this could be harmful to plants such as *A. filifera*. A very open soil must be used, and often they appear to thrive in a 'pot-bound' condition.

Aloe LILIACEAE

This is a genus recently reclassified within the family Asphodelaceae, and includes several hundred species, many of which are of sufficiently restricted growth and pleasing appearance to merit their inclusion as beginners' plants. *A. aristata* is the best-known of the genus, of easy culture, growing freely but never too big, offsetting to form groups, and flowering with spikes of reddish, lily-like blooms. This requires a sunny position, not too much water at any time, and is suitable for either house or greenhouse culture. Several other *Aloe* such as *A. variegata*, the partridge breasted aloe, with beautifully marked, triangular-shaped rosettes, are equally versatile. *A humilis* and its varietal forms are also desirable and easily grown plants, always of dwarf growth and free-flowering, preferably for greenhouse culture. If larger-growing species are required, the very popular *A. arborescens* is worthy of inclusion, being quick-growing, of easy culture, branching freely from the base to form substantial clusters, and bearing heavy spikes of deep orange-red flowers. Another plant, *A. striata*, sometimes called the coral aloe, is very showy, having grey-green leaves edged pink without marginal teeth and with a large head of flowers in late winter and early spring. There are many others with attractive features all of their own: *A. longistyla* is of medium growth, stemless with fleshy leaves, having spines on both surfaces and marginal teeth; its main attraction lies in the inflorescence, this being short and thick with a dense cluster of pinkish-red flowers.

Aloinopsis MESEMBRYANTHEMACEAE

This is a rather small genus of dwarf-growing, compact plants all of which grow in the form of clusters and have very fleshy roots. *A. schoonesii* is characteristic of most of the genus, very low-growing, leaves somewhat spoon-shaped and brownish-green in colour with unusual brownish-yellow flowers. It requires very arid conditions, no water at all in the resting season and only a moderate amount when in growth and flower. It makes a good companion in bowl-garden culture, especially with species of cacti whose rest season corresponds; or, of course, it can be grown equally successfully in the greenhouse, but always in a bright sunny position.

Aporocactus CACTACEAE

This is also a rather small genus of plants, sometimes referred to as rat's tail cactus. They are excellent subjects for hanging baskets or for a position where the long tails can fall naturally to give best effect, especially when in flower. *A. flagelliformis* is a popular species, originating from Mexico, with long, soft pendent stems or branches and brilliant rich crimson, long-lasting flowers. It prefers a bright, but not too sunny position in either the greenhouse or the home.

Astrophytum CACTACEAE

A small genus of unusual-shaped plants, each and every one is much sought after by collectors, beginners and specialists alike! It is typically a greenhouse group, of fairly easy culture, having conspicuously beautiful flowers, but demanding a thorough resting period from late autumn to late winter or early spring. The bishop's cap cactus, *A. myriostigma*, somewhat globular in shape with only few broad ribs and completely covered with whitish-grey scales, is native to parts of Mexico and has bright yellow flowers. *A. ornatum* has varying body colourings, green, grey or whitish, sometimes mottled, with wide fluted ribs, few spines and large deep yellow flowers with a reddish centre. Another less common species, *A. capricorne* has an oval-shaped body, many twisted spines of brownish-black and bears soft yellow terminal flowers with a rich orange-carmine throat. A well-grown plant of any of these species makes one of the most attractive specimens for any collector to possess.

Bowiea LILIACEAE

This is a most unusual plant with a large, onion-like bulbous base which is always exposed and only the roots penetrate the ground. It is a true succulent with long growth which dies down each year. *B. volubilis* is the best known of this very small genus, and is suitable for the greenhouse where it has the opportunity to climb; the flowers are small, green and appear towards the top of the stems. When growth begins to wither, water should be withheld until new growth recommences.

Caralluma ASCLEPIADACEAE

There are a great number of species in this genus, a few are very easy to grow, whilst many can prove exceedingly difficult and temperamental. *C. europaea* has very erect, grey-green, four-angled stems, often with minute reddish spots. Flowers are greenish-yellow with a brown centre, borne in umbels. Native to the Mediterranean countries, it is quite easy to grow, requiring a very open compost, with never too much water, and kept dry during dormancy; it is most suited to a sunny position in the greenhouse. *C. burchardii* is from the Canary Islands and has a grouping habit consisting of many bluish-green stems. Flowers are small, dark olive-green, covered with numerous whitish hairs which almost give the impression of a bluish flower! Again, this need offer no difficulty in greenhouse culture so long as it has a complete rest during dormancy and enjoys a bright, but not too sunny position.

Carpobrotus MESEMBRYANTHEMACEAE

One of the most readily recognized groups of succulent plants – some of which can be encountered growing outdoors in many parts of Europe, including Britain and naturalized in many sub-tropical countries. They are creeping, trailing plants with very succulent, thick leaves set opposite along the fleshy stems. These are smooth, often angled and bright-green in colour. Flowers are terminally borne. They are of easy culture, from either seeds or cuttings, and will accept cold house conditions in winter so long as they remain fairly dry. *C. edulis* from Natal is one of the best known. This develops stems to 2 m (6½ ft) long, somewhat angled – the leaves gradually tapering to a point, these often to 8 cm (3 in) long and over 1.2 cm (½ in) wide and thick. Flowers are large, bright yellow, but becoming pinkish later. *C. acinaciformis* is very similar – long trailing and spreading branches, greyish-green leaves about 9 cm (3½ in) long, some-times with a rough surface. Flowers are about 12 cm (4½ in) across and rich crimson-purple, opening after midday. This also is from Natal. This is a very widely distributed genus being found in many parts of South Africa and very distinctive species native only to Australia. One of the latter, *C. glaucescens*, has elongated stems to 2 m (6½ ft) long, slightly bluish-green leaves and flowers of pale purple or lilac with whitish area below. It is found mainly in New South Wales and Queensland.

Cephalocereus CACTACEAE

Once considered a very large genus, it is now reduced to only a small number. These are comparatively tall-growing plants which, when fully grown, develop a pseudocephalium consisting of a dense area of white bristles at the top and partially down the side of the plant. *C. senilis,* the old man cactus, is not too difficult to grow; it is of Mexican origin, from an area where there are prolonged periods of drought. Therefore it is important to give complete dryness during the winter months so as to avoid any tendency to rot, a problem which often affects hairy cacti. From almost germination time it has long white hair, this persisting throughout its life. Mature plants produce rose-pink flowers about 5 cm (2 in) long. Suitable only for greenhouse culture, it must be situated in a warm, sunny position.

Cereus CACTACEAE

All species are tall-growing, generally branching freely from the base and sides. As young plants, they can be used for bowl-garden work, but once they begin to grow well they are best transferred to a greenhouse, given a largish pot and allowed to develop more naturally. *C. peruvianus* is from South America, easy to grow and most attractive as a young plant. There is also a very attractive *monstrosus* form of the species and this is of equally easy culture. *C. jamacura* is very similar to it but differs in having bluish-green stems, whilst the former is dark-green. Neither is likely to flower until many years have passed and complete maturity is achieved. Flowers are nocturnal and pure white.

Ceropegia ASCLEPIADACEAE

Most species are of climbing or pendent habit, developing long trailing branches, these often arising from a tuberous root system. The flowers are the principal attraction, generally resembling miniature lanterns. All are relatively easy to grow and are best suited for greenhouse culture, requiring a fairly rich compost, a bright position and facilities to spread their branches to good effect. If a reasonably good temperature is maintained, plants will flourish the year through, but even so, beware of excess watering. *C. woodii,* which resembles a miniature ivy, is well known, having heart-shaped leaves of blue-green colour with whitish mottlings. The purple flower are small, slightly curved and expanding towards the tip, with the base quite bottle-shaped. *C. radicans* is a very succulent plant with long, dark green stems and large unusual flowers of purple, green and white. It is native to parts of Cape Province. The most succulent climbing species is possibly *C. stapeliaeformis,* which, as its name suggests, appears to have stems similar to those of *Stapelia*. Stems are thick, rounded, greyish-green with purple markings. Flowers have spreading lobes, the inner surface being white, the outer brownish with white spots.

Cheiridopsis MESEMBRYANTHEMACEAE

This is a large genus of easy growing plants, but requiring a very definite resting period, during which time the leaves dry back, protecting the new leaves by a kind of 'sleeve'. *C. pillansii* has very thick leaves and flowers during early summer. *C. candidissima* is an outstanding species, forming quite large clusters of whitish-green leaves and large pale-pink flowers. Essentially it is a greenhouse plant requiring full sun to produce the finest flowers. All species are native to South Africa.

Cleistocactus CACTACEAE

A very interesting genus with rather peculiar tubular flowers from which only the style and stamens protrude. The very attractive *C. strausii* with its white columnar-shaped stem is a 'must' for the beginner. It originates from Bolivia, and is by no means difficult to cultivate, possibly being most suited for the greenhouse, although as a young plant it is useful for bowl gardens. Given a bright position and careful watering, it makes quite rapid growth, eventually producing deep reddish flowers.

Of the other species, perhaps *C. brookei* (syn: *C. wendlandiorum*) deserves mention. This also is from Bolivia. A columnar species with slender stems, 22 ribs, and short yellowish spines arising from each areole. Flowers appear when plants are quite small, even at about 30 cm (12 in). These are more or less cylindrical, protruding horizontally from the stem, about 5 cm (2 in) long, red with yellowish tinges towards the base. Another popular species, *C. smaragdiflorus* has very spiny stems and bears flowers of red and green towards the top of the stems – these are tubular in shape, about 5 cm (2 in) long. This is from Paraguay, Argentina and Bolivia. All species are of easy culture.

Copiapoa CACTACEAE
A very exciting and 'different' group of plants originating from Chile. Most of the species are not readily available, so if the opportunity arises they should be purchased. None is particularly difficult to grow, requiring much the same conditions and requirements as most other genera from similar localities. They are definitely for greenhouses, where they should have full sunlight, ample moisture during the growing season but none during dormancy. Whilst the flowers are not large, they are very interesting. *C. cinerea* has a whitish-grey body, dense white wool at the apex, broad ribs with black spines and yellow flowers.

Coryphantha CACTACEAE
This genus has increased in popularity in recent times. In many ways the plants resemble those of *Mammillaria,* but in general, flowers are larger, appearing from the the axils of the tubercles from the crown of the plant. The spination also adds to their appeal, these mostly being quite long, often curved, several developing from each areole. They can be raised very successfully from seeds, although it may take 3–5 years before flowers appear regularly. Always provide a good sunny position. *C. poselgeriana* is from Coahuila, Mexico – a globular plant with a greyish-green body, 18–20 cm (7–8 in) high, symmetrically covered with very pronounced tubercles, each about 2.5 cm (1 in) wide at the base. Areoles from the tips of the tubercles produce up to seven straight brownish spines about 2 cm ($\frac{3}{4}$ in) long and a single white tipped central one twice as long as the radials. Flowers are pale yellowish or creamy-white with a red centre. *C. vivipara* is a transfer from *Escobaria,* and after many years is still referred to under that generic title. It comes from southern parts of Canada and a number of States of U.S.A. and in fact is almost hardy if kept dry in winter. It clusters freely and forms colonies of short semi-globular bodies of dark-green. Flowers are a purplish-red with slender, pointed petals about 5 cm (2 in) across. *C. bumamma* is a globular species bluish-green in colour covered by rounded tubercles – white woolly in the axils. Spines are about 2 cm ($\frac{3}{4}$ in) long, greyish-brown. Flowers

yellow with red throat, about 5 cm (2 in) wide. A Mexican species from Guerrero.

Crassula CRASSULACEAE
A very large and varied genus, most of which are well suited for those initially interested in growing succulents. *C. argentea,* the largest-growing of the genus, is very well known with its thick, almost bonsai-like trunk, and deep-green fleshy leaves; as a young plant it is often used in bowl gardens, and as a large, mature specimen it will be covered with pinkish-white flowers during many of the winter months in the greenhouse. *C. lycopodioides* resembles one of the club-mosses, having somewhat erect stems bearing numerous minute green leaves and equally small whitish flowers. *C. barbata* provides a very interesting and unusual plant, forming dense rosettes of deep-green leaves which are edged with numerous white hairs. Flowers are borne on an erect stalk and are whitish in colour. *C. rosularis* forms a basal rosette of very slender, waxy leaves and an erect inflorescence of many small white flowers. Occasionally the inflorescence becomes fasciated. These and many others can be satisfactorily grown by the amateur; the majority require a very bright position, especially the smaller-growing, densely-leaved types, and their rest season must be respected by keeping the plants quite dry. Most species are native to South Africa, particularly the succulent varieties, and are generally suited for greenhouse culture or the home.

Delosperma MESEMBRYANTHEMACEAE
A large genus of somewhat shrubby plants, many of which are almost unknown in cultivation. however, a few are very desirable and easy to grow, but to produce the best results a very sunny aspect is essential. *D. echinatum* is an attractive bushy plant with pale green, fleshy, oval leaves covered with bristly white papillae. The yellow flowers appear over a very long period. *D. steytlerae* is a dwarf species with very narrow, pointed leaves and white flowers. They originate from very arid country in South Africa where rain is scarce, hence a very porous, open soil is necessary and watering should be moderate at any time.

Dyckia BROMELIACEAE
These are terrestrial plants from a large family, most of which are totally epiphytic in nature. *D. sulphurea* has bright green leaves in the form of rosettes about 15 cm (6 in) in diameter, from the centre of which arises a long slender spike of sulphur yellow flowers. *D. rariflora* has dark green, narrow leaves with a long spike of deep orange flowers. These plants require a very light position and are suitable for either the home or the greenhouse. In general, a richer soil is needed than for other succulents,

This remarkable epiphyllum hybrid was developed in USA. '*King Midas*' is worthy of its common name '*The King of Gold*', flowers often exceeding 30 cm across.

This smaller flowering 'Queen Anne' is a choice, easily flowered house or greenhouse plant – very suited for hanging basket culture.

and a moist condition can be maintained throughout the year so long as a temperature of 10°C (50°F) is provided. Both species are from South America.

Echeveria CRASSULACEAE

Several members of this genus are very well known and popular plants, principally because of the varying forms of the rosettes with so many colourful shades of green, grey, red, brown, etc. The majority are native to Mexico, and with few exceptions can be counted among the most easy to cultivate. *E. elegans* is one of the smaller types with compact, white rosettes which offset very freely and form clusters. *E. derenbergii* is also a small rosette of pale green leaves, rather thickish, with red margins. Flowers are an added attraction, these being orange-yellow, borne in profusion on compact stems, and lasting for many weeks. *E. setosa* is a stemless species with rosettes of thick, hairy leaves and striking red and yellow flowers. *E. agavoides* has a much larger rosette than the foregoing, consisting of greyish-green, somewhat triangular-pointed leaves, with the suggestion of reddish margins. The flowers are reddish-yellow and borne on very long stems. *E. subrigida* is found on fairly high ground in central Mexico. It has a fairly dense rosette of rather flat bluish-green leaves and carries an inflorescence, often to 60 cm (2 ft) long tipped with several reddish or pinkish flowers. *E. rosea* grows epiphytically in nature and is found in the forests of eastern and central Mexico. A most fascinating plant with relatively small rosettes of deep-green leaves and a rather dense spike of rose-red flowers. Porous soil is a necessity, and given a sunny position it will flourish in either the greenhouse or on a bright window-ledge. Watering should be very restricted during the winter months unless a fairly good temperature is maintained.

Echinocactus CACTACEAE

Mainly large-growing, barrel-shaped plants, they carry through their own peculiar characteristics from soon after germination until maturity. *E. grusonii* is undoubtedly the outstanding species in the genus with its light green body, numerous ribs and golden yellow spines, justifying its common name of golden barrel. This is native to Mexico where it is exposed to full sunlight. This eye-catching species is best cultivated in the greenhouse where it should be given the brightest position possible. Ordinary cactus soil is ideal, but it must be very sandy; watering should cease throughout the resting season. Unfortunately flowers only develop on very mature plants, and this stage is only reached after many years when the plant is well over 30 cm (12 in) in diameter, but it is well worth cultivating for its distinctive golden body colouring. Incidentally, the flowers are fairly small and yellow in colour.

Echinocereus CACTACEAE

One of the most colourful genera of the Cactaceae, plants appear in many forms, some being roundish, others cylindrical, many clustering, whilst some remain solitary. Not all can be recommended for the beginner, but fortunately there are some which are very easy to cultivate. *E. blanckii* is representative of the more spreading species, with many slender, semi-erect stems and large, purplish-red flowers about 7 cm (3 in) in diameter in summer. The pectinate species have an added attraction: whilst the flowers are large and colourful, the body of the plant is completely covered by densely set, slender spines. *E. reichenbachii* is just one of the several species in this category, having large pink and white flowers. *E. fendleri* is a very variable species from USA and northern parts of Mexico. The spination differs considerably from one variety to another, equally so the flower colour. One of the most interesting and colourful was discovered in the Clark Mountains near the California/Nevada border – this has a large flower about 6.5 cm ($2\frac{1}{2}$ in) across, pale lilac-pink around the edges with a deep purple throat.

A sunny position is advised for most of the species; this helps in the production of flowers and in keeping the plant healthy. A rest period without water is essential, and, in general, extra humus in the soil mix is an advantage. All species are native to southern USA and Mexico.

Echinopsis CACTACEAE

This genus has now been increased by the merging of *Trichocereus* with its mainly tall-growing species. These, together with those already in the genus, are among best known cacti. All are very easy to grow and flower, and present no problems at all to the beginner. *E. multiplex* has many pronounced ribs and longish spines: it also groups freely, the offsets of which can be easily removed and established as separate plants. Flowers are large, lilac-pink and borne on a long tube. *E. eyriesii* is very similar, but with much shorter spines and large pure white flowers. Often hybrids of these two are available, and this often means that characteristics of both species are to be seen, especially with regard to flower colour; hence a plant looking like *E. eyriesii* in body shape develops a lilac-coloured flower and vice versa. The smaller globular species of *Echinopsis* have been used most successfully in producing many colourful hybrids. These, in the main, retain the body characteristics of the 'mother' plant, *Echinopsis*, and having been cross-pollinated with species of *Lobivia*, result in many beautifully coloured blooms being developed. Colours in varying shades of yellow, orange, pink and red, even multi-coloured have become available, and, in general, the flowers are longer lasting than those of the parent species.

The taller growing plants originally within *Trichocereus* include nocturnal flowering *E. spachianus*, with densely spined green stem, which produces delightful, attractive large white trumpet-shaped flowers from its densely spined, bristly areoles, usually set around the crown of the plant. Of similar habit is *E. macrogonus*, an elegant, erect plant with a bluish-green stem, sometimes branching from the base, bearing equally large pure white nocturnal flowers. *E. smrzianus* is another tall-growing species transferred from *Trichocereus*. It is native of northern Argentina. A densely spined plant, similar in some respects to *E. spachianus*, with about the same number of ribs – brownish-yellow spines but with flowers 12 cm ($4\frac{1}{2}$ in) long and wide. These appear towards the tips of the stems, white, with slightly pinkish outer segments. *E. candicans* is quite a fast growing species from north-west Argentina. It can attain 1 m ($3\frac{1}{4}$ ft) in height and about 16 cm ($6\frac{1}{2}$ in) thick, with up to 11 ribs, long radial and central spines – the latter to 10 cm (4 in) in length. Flowers are nocturnal, pure white, about 20 cm (8 in) long – and they have a lily-like scent. Young plants of these two, together with *E. pachanoi* make excellent grafting-stock for more temperamental seedlings of other genera. Plants can grow to substantial proportions and make splendid specimens, but the general requirements for most cacti must apply. These are of South American origin and are suitable for general cultivation.

Epiphyllum CACTACEAE

Reference has been made to species and hybrids of this genus in an earlier chapter. Many excellent subjects for both greenhouse and home culture are to be found here; the botanic species are in themselves most attractive, although the majority are nocturnal flowering, but sweetly scented. The hybrids or 'cultivars' offer an even greater range than has already been indicated, and if flowers are the main consideration, then no group within the Cactaceae can offer an assortment of more colour and charm. *E. hookeri* has elongated, pale green flattened stems with pronounced marginal crenations; the flowers are white, about 15 cm (6 in) diameter, with many thin slender petals and a long style of 15 cm (6 in) or more in length, rich purplish magenta with shades of orange towards the tip of the base, this being one of its distinguishing features. This is crowned with fourteen deep yellow lobes. It is a native of Trinidad and parts of South America. *E. crenatum* from Central America is a parent of many of the cultivars available today. The stems are flat but thick, deeply crenated on the margins and the large, day-flowering, creamy-white blooms about 15 cm (6 in) in diameter are sweetly scented. *E. oxypetalum* is a most popular houseplant in the USA, sometimes called the Dutchman's pipe on account of the long curved tube of the flower. The stems are

Ferocactus emoryi tends to remain globular in shape in cultivation and will readily produce flowers. In the wild it develops semi-giant proportions.

rather thin, bright green, with wavy margins. Flowers are nocturnal, very large and creamy-white in colour. A fairly rich soil is best for these epiphytic types, and if a reasonable temperature is maintained, they should not be allowed to go completely dry at any time. Position-wise, they do not require full sun; a somewhat shaded, but not dark, position is preferred. Many beautiful cultivars have been mentioned elsewhere, and much the same requirements are necessary to grow and flower these to perfection.

Espostoa CACTACEAE

These plants of columnar habit develop, in maturity, a pseudocephalium. It is a beautiful genus, most species of which have white hairs and bright, longish spines. As young plants they can be used for bowl gardens or other home decoration, but are best removed to the greenhouse as they become larger. A certain amount of lime is an advantage – this can be included in the soil mixture – and the whiteness of the plant will benefit in consequence. *E. lanata* is one of the finest and better known: it originates from Peru at high altitudes. The stem is covered with white hairs and brownish, needle-like spines which are apparent from quite an early age. In maturity, small reddish flowers are produced from the pseudocephalium.

Euphorbia EUPHORBIACEAE

This is considered to be one of the largest plant families on record. The succulent species are particularly fascinating because of the numerous shapes and sizes of the extremely fleshy varieties. Some are undoubtedly beginners' plants, and so long as watering is restricted to the minimum, no great difficulty will be encountered. Soil must be very porous, and wherever possible, a bright, airy position should be provided. To mention or even select a few suitable species would be a great task, but there are a number which are sought after for their own peculiarities. *E. obesa* is such a plant, and could easily be mistaken for certain cacti species. A spherical, broadly ribbed plant, it is very attractively marked with reddish-brown and dark green lines, almost plaid-like. It originates from Cape Province in South Africa; it is imperative that water is withheld in winter months, or for that matter at any time when a temperature of 10°C (50°F) cannot be maintained as any retention of moisture in low temperature conditions quickly leads to rot. *E. milii*, better known as *E. splendens*, the crown of thorns, is one of the best to grow. Generally a shrubby plant with many spines and leaves, it bears numerous bright red flowers over a long period. This is an excellent houseplant, but always needs a bright position and ample water when in growth and flower. *E. ingens* is a tree species, but, as a young plant, can be used satisfactorily for the home. The dark green, mottled foliage gives a pleasing appearance throughout its life, and it proves to be of easy culture, even in maturity. It is best to get guidance from specialist nurseries as to which of the many species are best suited for your conditions: there are many which are relatively easy to grow; look out for *E. flanaganii*, *E. caput-medusae*, *E. polygona* as they are well worth obtaining.

Faucaria MESEMBRYANTHEMACEAE

These delightful miniature species are all of compact growth, with a somewhat rosette leaf formation. Leaves are very fleshy, generally with several marginal teeth. Very suitable for either greenhouse or home culture, their main requirement is to restrict the moisture during the rest season. *F. tigrina* is called tiger's jaws; the leaves are thick, flattened on the upper surface, rounded on the lower and tapering towards the tip. The leaves are also keeled at the tip, forming a small 'chin'. The combination of the greyish-green foliage with their toothed margins and the brilliant golden yellow flowers makes this one of the most beautiful of the genus. There are others which have equally attractive characteristics. A lesser-known species, but no more difficult to cultivate is *F. candida* which gives white flowers.

Ferocactus CACTACEAE

This is an imposing genus of fairly large-growing plants, heavily spined and free flowering in maturity. As young plants they are globular in shape, but several become more barrel-shaped after many years. All are of easy culture, requiring a very porous soil, a bright sunny position and ample water throughout the growing season. They are primarily for greenhouse culture. *F. latispinus* has a somewhat depressed crown and is fiercely spined; these spines offer an easy method of identification, developing from a large areole, with about eight to ten pinkish-white radial spines, about four thicker centrals and one of these decidedly thick, wide and hooked, and pinkish-brown in colour. Flowers are purple, the species being of Mexican origin. *F. acanthodes*, which is found in several areas of southern USA and Mexico, is more spine-covered than the previous species; these spines are reddish or yellow in colour, and densely and tortuously twisted in all directions. The flowers are yellowish-orange. *F. fordii* is one of the smaller species, native of Baja California, and produces a ring of pinkish-rose flowers around the crown.

  F. emoryi, originally known as *F. covillei*, is one of the most spectacular species to be seen in Sonora, Mexico, as well as in southern parts of Arizona. It is a large somewhat globular-cylindrical plant, often growing in quite dense scrubland, to over 2 m ($6\frac{1}{2}$ ft) tall with over 30 ribs, the areoles with up to 8 radial spines and one longer central, reddish-brown in colour. Flowers are borne in the crown of the plant, about 6 cm ($2\frac{1}{2}$ in) long, deep yellowish-orange or yellowish-red. *F. gracilis* is rather similar in some respects, but of shorter growth, rarely exceeding 1 m ($3\frac{1}{4}$ ft) in height. It has about 20 ribs, the areoles with 12–14 radial spines of pale yellow and about 9 central reddish spines to 7 cm ($2\frac{3}{4}$ in) long, one of which is frequently curved at the tip. Flowers are only about 4 cm ($1\frac{1}{2}$ in) long, at the crown of the plant, dull yellowish in colour with a red median line. This is native of Baja California.   These and others offer splendid scope for the enthusiast and can be recommended. The emphasis is on a sunny position; without this the colour attraction of the spination will be lost.

Gasteria LILIACEAE

From the point of view of nomenclature, this is probably one of the most difficult of genera to determine. This is another genus now considered to belong to the family Asphodelaceae. So many hybrids have become readily available over the years that confusion has resulted in true naming. Hybrids or otherwise, most species are very good plants for either house or greenhouse, and in the majority of instances have most attractively marked foliage. G. *verrucosa* is one of the best known, with leaves about 15 cm (6 in) or more in length, arranged in two rows, their surfaces totally covered with small tubercles, giving an overall greyish appearance. G. *maculata* has dark green, glossy leaves 20 cm (8 in) long and very wide, with a broadly pointed tip; towards the tips the leaves are marked with whitish spots in bands. Several other species can be recommended: G. *armstrongii* with thick glaucous leaves, mostly prostrate and forming a thick rosette; G. *liliputana*, one of the smallest of the genus, has serrated leaf-margins and is marked with greenish-white spots, with a definite keel on the underside of each leaf. They prosper in almost any soil, and while they tend to flourish on neglect, a little careful attention will help produce the finest of results.

Glottiphyllum MESEMBRYANTHEMACEAE

This is another popular genus, many species of which have very similar characteristics; it is sometimes difficult to tell one from another. Careful watering is an essential requirement; too much water will encourage the plant to grow out of character, the leaves becoming elongated and soft. A long, dry resting season is therefore necessary, together with a very sunny aspect, so the brightest position in the greenhouse is to be recommended. G. *longum* has bright green leaves, but distinctly tinted reddish if the most suitable position is afforded. Flowers are yellow and daisy-like. G. *album* has most characteristics the same as the foregoing, but the flowers are pure white. These and most of the others are equally easy to grow, all requiring the same conditions.

Gymnocalycium CACTACEAE

This is one of the most popular of genera, all globular in shape, with ribs divided into tubercles. Flowers are somewhat bell-shaped, the tube being covered with broad scales with naked axils, a main characteristic of the genus. Whilst they should be rested during the coldest months, when the growing season commences ample watering is required. During the warmest months, the plants should have a certain amount of protection from full sun. Given a bright position indoors, they will flourish as houseplants, but greenhouse culture is to be preferred. G. *mihanovitchii* has a plaid-like colouring with sharp ribs and transverse bands above and below the areoles. Flowers are greenish-yellow. The brightly coloured grafted plants of red, yellow, white and orange are frequently of this species (see earlier reference). *G. saglione* is one of the largest in the genus; the 'chins' (tubercles) are very prominent, from which are produced red or greyish curved spines. Flowers are pinkish-white. A number of new discoveries have been made in recent years, especially in southern Brazil. *G. horstii* and the *var. bueneckeri* are two examples. They have glossy green stems with 5–6 rather bumpy ribs, relatively few spines and large pinkish or creamy flowers about 10 cm (4 in) across. The variety always bears fairly deep pink blooms. All are native of South America.

Haageocereus CACTACEAE

Most species have golden spines, but the method of growth varies tremendously. Some are somewhat columnar, others clambering or semi-erect. These are all typically greenhouse plants, requiring good sunlight, dry resting season, and moderate watering in the growing season. A rich, open compost is needed for best results. *H. decumbens* has sprawling growth, the stems being almost completely covered with golden

The clustering habit of *Huernia kirkii* is considerably enhanced by the exotic flowers which appear at ground level around the circumference of the plant.

spines. The flowers are whitish. *H. versicolor* has slender, erect growth, densely ribbed with numerous reddish-brown and yellow spines. Both species are native to Peru. These are most attractive throughout their lives, the brilliance of the spination never diminishing.

Hatiora CACTACEAE

These are dainty bushy plants, spineless, the stems consisting of numerous small, somewhat bottle-shaped, segments. It is only a small genus, and all are epiphytic in their native Brazil. *H. salicornioides* has dark-green joints and bears bright, yellowish-orange flowers. *H. bambusioides* is very similar, but with longer joints which are clavate in shape. Flowers appear at the terminal ends of the joints, bright orange in colour.

Hatiora has received several additions to its species in recent years. A new discovery – *H. herminiae* with small, rather more cylindrical segments has areoles with 1–2 bristles. Flowers are a rich deep pink, about 2 cm ($\frac{3}{4}$ in) long – a departure from previously known species which only boasted of orange shades. The genus *Pseudozygocactus* has become merged with *Hatiora* – thus the solitary species and its variety now have a new generic title! *H. epiphylloides* from Sao Paulo in Brazil has small, fleshy segments to about 2.5 cm (1 in) long, in some ways similar to those of *Rhipsalidopsis rosea*, but slightly notched with small bare areoles. There is also *var. bradei* which has much smaller segments, rarely exceeding 1.2 cm ($\frac{1}{2}$ in) long, certainly club-shaped, but more flat. Flowers are yellowish in species and variety, borne at the terminal ends of the branches. This is one of several epiphytic rarities which tend to prosper if grafted on to more robust stock – in this instance, *Selenicereus rostratus* has proved invaluable.

Very suited for either house or greenhouse, they require shade for best results with ample watering during the growing season; they should never be allowed to go completely dry when dormant. A rich compost is a necessity, but this must nevertheless be very porous.

Haworthia LILIACEAE

This is a very interesting, low-growing genus of leaf succulents; the attraction lies mainly in the varied leaf markings and shapes as the flowers are somewhat uninteresting and very similar to one another. The majority can be classified as being suitable for house decor or the greenhouse. Overall, they prefer a somewhat shady position, although just a few improve their leaf colouring if exposed moderately to the sun. They need only a short resting season, when water should be withheld, but throughout the warmest months liberal watering is beneficial. *H. attenuata* has a rosette of narrow, attenuate leaves with cross rows of numerous white tubercles. *H. reinwardtii* is also a highly decorative plant, with many whitish tubercles and rosette shapes generally different from most other species, and it groups readily from the base. *H. tessellata* has hard leaves of deep greyish-green, tessellated on the glossy leaf surfaces. *H. retusa* is one of the 'window' species, the upper portions of the leaves seem as if they have been bent over at right-angles, this portion being flat or retuse and forming the windows. *H. setata* is unusual in its leaf structure and represents a few other species with similar characteristics, such as *H. bolusii*. The leaves are edged with small bristle-like teeth; this is particularly noticeable with *H. setata var. gigas* where the whole plant looks extremely fluffy and whitish-hairy. For the beginner, there are few other genera to match *Haworthia* for simplicity in growing, and its adaptability to almost any reasonable conditions. This is also now a member of the family Asphodelaceae.

Hoya ASCLEPIADACEAE
This is a well-known genus, many species of which are very succulent and of fairly easy culture. The majority are of climbing habit, although a few tend to remain short and rather short and rather bush-like. *H. carnosa* is undoubtedly the best known, having been used for house and greenhouse decoration over many years. The pinkish, wax-like flowers are very fragrant and carried in umbels. There are varieties of the species: *var. compacta* has short growth and twisted, curled leaves; *var. exotica* has green leaves, mottled and edged yellow; *var. variegata* has green leaves variegated white. *H. bella* is representative of the dwarfer-growing species, somewhat bush-like with straight stems, small, thick leaves and white flowers with purple centres. A number of very attractive species are becoming generally available, which, whilst bearing some resemblance to the better known species, have particular appeal. *H. cinnamomifolia* from Indonesia is a climbing plant with almost fleshy, ovate leaves, the margins slightly recurved. It gets its title because the shape and colour of the leaves resemble those of the Cinnamon tree – *Cinnamomum zeylanicum*. Flowers are in hemispherical umbels – a rotate corolla of yellowish-green and the corona segments deep purple-red. *H. purpurea-fusca* comes from the island of Java. This is also a climber with dark-green, somewhat glossy leaves speckled with silver. Leaves are ovate-lanceolate, to 8 cm (3 in) long, set opposite along the trailing branches. Flowers are in large umbels of many individual blooms of reddish-purple or purplish-brown. A temperature of 15°C (59°F) should be maintained for good results. One, possibly the most dwarf species, deserves mention – *H. engleriana* from Thailand, a succulent epiphytic plant. Leaves are small, only a matter of 1.5 cm ($\frac{5}{8}$ in) long and 4 mm ($\frac{1}{8}$ in) wide, the upper surface convex, wax-like and deep-green. Flowers are in very

small umbels, usually four-together, carried at the terminal ends of the slender branches – a white corolla which glistens with a deep violet corona. It wants a very bright position but not full sun.

Huernia ASCLEPIADACEAE

This is quite a large genus of mainly South African plants, closely related to the *Stapelia*. All species are not necessarily easy to cultivate, so care should be taken in selection. A temperature of 10°C (50°F) should be maintained throughout the rest season with no watering whatsoever. Too much sun or shade can be equally damaging to the plants, so every effort must be made to find the happy medium. These can only be recommended for greenhouse culture. A very open, somewhat rich compost should be provided. *H. primulina* has creamy-white, wax-like flowers with an almost black corona at the base of the flower. *H. zebrina* is a clustering species, stems are angled, tapering towards the tip and

Kalanchoe rhombopilosa is one of the more miniature species of Madagascan *Kalanchoe* species. The speckled foliage is always very much in evidence.

flecked red. Flowers appear on short stalks, rather small, yellow with purple transverse bands. A somewhat taller species, *H. schneideriana* has angled, toothed stems and bell-shaped flowers, velvety-black on the inner surface, brownish on the outer, the lobes being decidedly recurved. *H. kirkii* from Transvaal is another clustering plant with stems to about 4 cm (1½ in) high and fascinating flowers whose yellow lobes are spotted red with deep purple corona.

Kalanchoe CRASSULACEAE

Some species become well-established as houseplants, mostly cultivars of *K. blossfeldiana* which have flowers of varying shades of red and purple. The true species has red flowers, dark green glossy leaves, edged red, and rather crenated towards the tip. It is a native of Madagascar. *K. marmorata* is another species sometimes used for home decor. It comes from Somalia and Kenya. A semi-shrubby plant with more or less erect stems and

Lampranthus species are ideal for pot or hanging-basket culture, flowering over a long period in late spring and early summer.

branching from base. Leaves are obovate to about 10 cm (4 in) long, greyish-green, pruinose – both surfaces marked with brownish blotches resembling marbling. Flowers white. *K. manginii* is also from Madagascar – it is very much a pendent species with woody creeping and trailing branches, very well suited for hanging basket culture and indoor decor. Leaves are small, to 3 cm (1¼ in) long, more or less oval in shape, quite thick and fleshy, and at an early stage quite hairy. Flowers are particularly attractive – reddish-orange, bell-shaped, to 2 cm (¾ in) long – each branch bearing several blooms. *K. tubiflora* is probably the best known of all – it was for long known as a *Bryophyllum*. It can reach 1 m (3¼ ft) in height – a robust plant, very erect, bearing cylindrical leaves of greyish-green spotted with brownish-red to about 10 cm (4 in) long, the tips notched from where appear adventitious buds. These eventually fall, root and establish as mature plants. The inflorescence carries red to purplish flowers in a fairly compact cluster. This is endemic to S. Madagascar.

K. *tomentosa* is also popular, the leaves being covered with whitish felt, generally spoon-shaped, tipped blackish or brown. There are varieties of this, some with quite large, whiter leaves, and one with very small foliage, deeply marked brown towards the apex. This is also from Madagascar and is ideally suited to home or greenhouse. *K. rhombopilosa* has now become well known and sought after, very distinctive with its small erect growth and miniature branches. The leaves are greyish-green with silver and red markings. The yellow flowers are small and seem to be rather timid in developing. However, it is a very beautiful species, best suited for the greenhouse. A bright position is advisable; not direct sun. Rest well when dormant, but water freely in the growing season. Open soil is needed.

Lampranthus MESEMBRYANTHEMACEAE

Mostly these are shrubby plants with either an erect or spreading habit. All species are of easy culture and have colourful flowers; in fact there are some which can be used for summer bedding in more privileged parts of Britain. All require full sunlight, so the preference is for greenhouse culture. Open porous soil is needed, with regular watering in the growing season. Keep plants dry in dormancy, although if a good temperature is maintained, they will take water the whole year through. *L. roseus* has the most vivid red or pink flowers with yellow centres, the habit of the plant being bushy and spreading. *L. aurantiacus* is an outstandingly beautiful species, fairly tall-growing and only sparsely branched, but during the flowering period it can become almost smothered with rich orange flowers. This applies equally to *L. purpureus* with its rough, bluish-green leaves and masses of pinkish-purple flowers. *L. conspicuus* has thickish prostrate stems; leaves are green with reddish tips and the flowers are rich red-purple with creamy centres. These and all the others in the genus are equally beautiful, but can be space-consuming when they mature to large plants.

Lepismium CACTACEAE

This is another small genus of epiphytes, closely allied to *Rhipsalis*, their separation based on the sunken 'ovary' in the stem margins; otherwise they are very similar. *L. cruciforme* and the varieties *anceps, myosurus, cavernosum* and *vollii* are among the better known, and these make excellent hanging-basket plants. Stems are triangular, except for the sometimes flattened stems of *var. anceps*. The predominant stem colouring is reddish-purple; flowers are either pink or white followed by purple fruits. A rich compost is necessary: plenty of leafmould in the mixture will produce excellent results. If they are to be used for hanging-baskets, it is recommended that the whole base of the basket is first covered completely with moss and charcoal chippings, so as to avoid the soil washing away through the open wire mesh. All are native to the South American rain-forests.

Lithops MESEMBRYANTHEMACEAE

These are fascinating little plants, resembling round pebbles; the generic title actually means 'like-stones'. Flowers are either white or yellow, but the plant surfaces have many differing marks, and this basically encompasses the seventy to eighty species. All are as easy as one another to cultivate, but great care most be exercised to ensure they have a correct dormant season, from early winter to late spring. The more popular of the yellow flowering species are *L. olivacea,* an olive-green plant with green 'windows' which clusters freely; *L. leslei* with a brownish-red or brownish-green body superimposed with a network of reddish-brown lines; *L. comptonii,* another fine example, the body becoming a rich wine colour if exposed to full sun. The white flowered species include *L. bella* with somewhat rounded tops, brownish in colour, and slightly grooved with many darker markings; *L. fulleri* with a greyish body and brownish markings, readily forming clusters. An essentially sunny position must be provided; the soil must be very sandy and porous; never overwater. All species change their outer 'skin' each year, and until this dried skin is shed, no watering at all is needed. These fascinating plants are all of South African origin.

Lobivia CACTACEAE

Somewhat slow-growing plants, these are more or less globose and many

Lampranthus aurantiacus is just one depicting the several brilliant colour forms of flowers within this genus, often obliterating the foliage!

All *Mammillaria* species are easy flowering and *M. mainae* is certainly no exception, producing its flowers from mid-spring to early summer.

Notocactus purpureus is one of the most colourful species from South Brazil and has only reached cultivation in more recent times.

species cluster freely. They are closely related to *Echinopsis* and it seems very likely the two genera will be merged. Hybrids between the two genera have produced some of the finest and richest coloured 'desert' cacti. A rich soil is necessary and regular watering throughout the warmest months; given a bright position, the flowers will enrich any greenhouse collection. All species are native to South America. *L. pentlandii* has a greyish-green body with about twelve ribs and brownish, back-curving spines and small, 'funnel-shaped', reddish-orange flowers. *L. hertrichiana* represents the smaller-growing species, scarcely ever offsetting in habitat, but in cultivation seeming to adopt this habit. The well-known peanut cactus, *Chamaecereus* is currently included as a *Lobivia*. *L. silvestri* is an Argentinian plant which has hairy peanut-like stems and bright orange-red flowers. To get best flowers, provide a really sunny position. Plants have glossy-green bodies and brilliant scarlet flowers. There are others which could be mentioned, but they are less frequently encountered.

Mammillaria CACTACEAE

One of the most popular genera represented by over 200 different species, it is native to Mexico, southern parts of the USA and certain West Indian islands. They differ enormously in their body structure; some remain solitary, whilst others offset very freely, forming almost inseparable clumps. Flowers are mostly quite small, but they appear over a long period, usually in great numbers, then followed by the red, pink or orange fruits which add distinction to the plant for a long while. By no means difficult to grow, their essential requirement of a completely dry dormancy must be provided. Good sun and reasonable watering in the growing season will help produce the best results. There are many species to choose from. Some are of more recent introduction, and they appear as easy to grow as those with which we have become so familiar. *M. elongata* has several forms, with spines differing in colour – white, yellow, brown and even deeper brown. The body is short and cylindrical and quickly develops into erect clusters. Flowers are whitish or yellowish-cream. *M. candida* is usually of solitary growth, only rarely caespitose. It is a Mexican plant, somewhat globular in shape, often growing to 8 cm (3 in) or more in diameter, with numerous white spines almost covering the body, and pink flowers. *M. mainae* is very attractive, native to an area from Nogales to Hermisillo in Mexico, where it is invariably found under the protection of scrub. The stem is globose, frequently clustering. The usually dark green tubercles have about ten radial spines, yellow, tipped brown, and widely spreading. The few central spines are distinctly hooked. The vivid, cerise-coloured flowers of *M. microcarpa* are in sharp contrast to *M. hahniana,* sometimes known as the old lady cactus, which is generally of solitary habit and often reaches 13 cm (5 in) or more in height. Spines are white and have numerous flexible, white bristly hairs. The red flowers appear as a crown around the top of the plant. *M. centri-cirrha* rapidly develops large clusters of dark green, somewhat rounded stems, the new growth developing in the crown of the plant in the form of dense whitish spines. Flowers are whitish or pinkish-white, followed by elongated deep red fruits, these persisting for many weeks. Others, such as *M. gracilis,* of clustering habit with numerous white-to-pink flowers; *M. zeilmanniana,* also of clustering habit and purplish-red flowers; and *M. spinosissima* so liable to be confused with *M. rhodantha. M. bocasana* is well known and still very popular. A number of genera have been merged with *Mammillaria* recently, including *Cochemiea.* One species included is *M. poselgeri,* probably one of the most glamorous, with rich flame-red flowers from near the crown of the plant. These are just a few of a host of interesting species which can provide the newcomer to the hobby with endless pleasure and enjoyment, yet at the same time he will experience the minimum of difficulty in growing them.

Monvillea CACTACEAE

This is a small genus of South American plants, all with slender, erect stems, and flowers that open at night. They are reasonably easy to grow, but generally speaking are best kept for greenhouse culture. A somewhat acid soil is preferable, but porous notwithstanding. If a fairly high temperature is maintained, water can still be given in moderation during the resting season. *M. spegazzini* has unusually bluish stems, marbled grey and white, mostly triangled with very pronounced tubercles, deep black spines and whitish-pink flowers. Very good light is necessary, but not full sun.

Myrtillocactus CACTACEAE

This embraces a few very beautiful species of Mexican origin, of rather 'bushy' habit, in that the branches form a thick, heavily massed growth of short, bluish-green trunk and branches, five to six angled. Areoles are set well apart and these are armed with black spines. Flowers appear only on mature plants, dull creamy-yellow in colour, followed by bluish fruits. *M geometrizens* and *M. cochal* have very much in common; both will prove good subjects for a beginner's greenhouse if the conditions set out in an earlier chapter are rigidly adhered to. They want to be not too cold, and not too dry, so this means a reasonably high winter temperature of 10°C (50°F).

A species which still has no definite habitat. *Opuntia bergeriana*, which is named in honour of the famous botanist of that name, remains an outstanding example of red-flowering opuntias.

Nananthus MESEMBRYANTHEMACEAE
This rather small genus of tuberous-rooted plants has distinctive leaves generally covered with minute white dots. *N. vittatus* has leaves 2.5 cm (1 in) long, narrow and triangular. The surface is rough with numerous dots. Flowers are rather small and yellow. *N. aloides* is a clumping species; the upper surface of the leaves is grooved, keeled towards the tips, and dark green dotted with many white spots. Flowers appear on a short stalk, yellow in colour. All species are native to South Africa. A bright sunny position is best for these plants; this brings out the colouring in the leaves and encourages flowering. A fairly rich, very open soil should be used; water must be withheld in the dormant season. They are best for greenhouse culture, and no difficulty should be encountered in growing them to perfection so long as the rules are kept. The other species, such as *N. transvaalensis* and *N. rubrolineatus,* will be equally satisfactory plants for the purpose.

Neoporteria CACTACEAE
This genus primarily includes species native to Chile. All are globular

plants with flowers appearing from near the crown. They are not difficult to grow, but as they flower during the colder months of the year in the northern hemisphere, it is necessary to maintain a temperature conducive to their requirements – nothing less than 13°C (55°F) for safety. A really sunny aspect is essential, so possibly the greenhouse will prove the better area in which to grow them. *N. fusca* is dark green having about twelve ribs, with tubercles and areoles armed with about eleven brownish spines; flowers are yellow. Several other species have been recorded under the generic titles of *Neochilenia* and *Islaya,* but these are all now merged within *Neoporteria.* There are several other species, sometimes appearing under *Chilenia* or *Nichelia;* in most cases the flowers are yellow.

Nopalea CACTACEAE

This is a genus related to the *Opuntia,* the main reason for their separation lying in the flower structure, the style and stamens being considerably longer than the closely adpressed petals. The tendency is for them to grow tall, but undoubtedly they can be useful to the beginner, especially for greenhouse culture. *N. cochenillifera* has rounded, smooth flat joints with few, if any, spines. It is dark glossy green in colour with the tubercles shaded brownish, flowers orange-red with pink stamens, and green stigma lobes. *N. dejecta* has bright green, elongated joints, tending to have a drooping effect, hence their specific title. The joints have whitish-yellowish spines and orange flowers at the tips of the joints. It is native to Mexico and Central America. It will be found that the joints are very brittle, breaking away from the main stem very easily; these can be set in open compost to provide further plants. A porous soil is necessary, but species tend to thrive without too much fertilizer. Full sun is beneficial with moderate watering at all times except during the main period of dormancy.

Nopalxochia CACTACEAE

A small genus of epiphytic plants, native to Mexico. It is ideally suited for greenhouse or home culture, the main requirements being a rich, open compost and a minimum temperature of 10°C (50°F); this should be increased as the plants come into bud and flower, otherwise buds will drop. A rather shady position is needed, but somewhat bright nevertheless. *N. phyllanthoides* is the best known, and parent of the improved strain 'Deutsche Kaiserin'. The habit is pendent, flowers appearing in early spring onwards in shades of pink, and lasting for many days. Keep the temperature correct, and then water can be given moderately throughout the year, but never give them 'wet feet'. *N. ackermannii* has very similar habit, but with red flowers.

Notocactus CACTACEAE

This is a very well-known, popular genus of South American origin. There is little difficulty in growing these satisfactorily, and many are equally successful either in the home or in the greenhouse, but a bright sunny position must be provided. Soil must be rich and open, and regular systematic watering during the growing season is required. Species differ considerably; some have a rather columnar shape, whilst most are globular, and many offset freely. *N. ottonis* and its varieties are clustering plants, with bright green bodies, ten to fifteen ribs, areoles with yellowish-brown or reddish spines, and golden yellow flowers with a reddish centre. *N. leninghausii* has a pale green, somewhat columnar body, with densely set areoles bearing numerous golden-yellow spines. The apex is rather flattened and slanted – a natural characteristic and not due to wrong growing. Flowers are large, golden-yellow, arising from the crown of the plant. Others of equal charm include *N. mammulosus* which is armed with many interlocking spines and golden-yellow flowers; *N. scopa* which is similar to *N. leninghausii* in form but without the slant, the spines being generally white, many with reddish or brownish tips, and the flowers borne in a ring near the crown; and *N. rutilans* which has an elongated, bluish-green body, brownish-red tipped spines and pale purple flowers. *N purpureus* has large vivid reddish-purple flowers and is one of the most sought-after plants within this genus of easily flowered cacti.

Opuntia CACTACEAE

One of the larger genera of cacti, this includes plants of many shapes and varying sizes drawn from many parts of the New World. The often tree-like form of many is very familiar to most people, also the round pad-like growth of the branches which often typifies a cactus. The majority, particularly as young plants, are ideal subjects for those commencing the hobby; a few might be useful for the home, but in general greenhouse culture is to be preferred. Only a short selection can have a place here, but each represents many other similar species of equal worth. *O. microdasys* is perhaps the best-known of all, often mentioned as the bunnies'-ears cactus, with oval pads set with areoles 'polka-dot' fashion, each with many sharp-bristly glochids, some yellow, or brownish-red (*var. rufida*) or white (*var. alba*). All are native to Mexico. More spiny and with more vicious glochids is *O. aciculata* and its *var. orbiculata;* both have thick, almost round pads densely covered with areoles, bearing sharp, yellowish-brown glochids and reddish flowers. This makes a splendid eyecatching specimen, one which is now considered extinct in its original USA habitat. *O. bergeriana* is another good red-flowering species. Its pad-like segments are pale green with few areoles, each with 3–5 yellowish grey spines. This plant's original habitat is still unknown. *O. leptocaulis* and its *var. longispina* are native to Mexico with slender, pencil-thick stems and branches, forming almost impenetrable thickets in its own surroundings but a Christmas-tree effect in cultivation if grown carefully. Flowers are small and greenish-yellow. Also with round, cylindrical stems is *O. tunicata,* not an easy plant to handle but very impressive with its long, silvery sharp spines. *O. subulata* is a tall-growing species with cylindrical stems, but no ribs. Fleshy leaves develop on new growth, but these very soon fall away; flowers are orange-yellow. *O. cylindrica* is very similar in appearance, but with sharp spines and reddish flowers. There are also many more miniature species which have a low, spreading habit and perhaps are better contained within the limits of a normal greenhouse. *O. verschaffeltii* has short, bright green stems and branches, sparsely spined, and reddish flowers. *O. pulchella* has small elliptical joints with whitish spines and deciduous glochids; flowers are pink to purple. Many more could be mentioned, but it is a matter of trying as many as available.

Oreocereus CACTACEAE

This is a small genus of columnar plants, native to Peru, Chile and Bolivia. The spination makes them ornamental and outstanding, and in general they offer very few problems in growing successfully. *O. celsianus* is a cylindrical species with heavy areoles bearing many yellowish spines and long brownish-white hairs. More mature plants tend to develop new growth from the base, and in maturity they will flower from the top of the branches, the flowers being deep red in colour. *O. trollii* is now considered a variety of *O. celsianus;* it is one of the most beautiful of cacti, being almost completely covered with longish white hairs and wool, the long, slender yellow spines protruding almost horizontally from the body of the plant. Flowers on mature plants are rich carmine red, and day-flowering. A certain amount of lime in the compost could prove beneficial, but above all it must be very porous. Water moderately in the growing season, and keep completely dry in dormancy. The location should be a sunny position, hence greenhouse culture might be preferable.

Orostachys CRASSULACEAE

A peculiarly unusual genus, its origin lies in much cooler areas, mainly China and certain other areas of Eastern Asia. Perhaps these are not too readily available, but are well worth seeking after as they are easy to cultivate, pleasing to the eye, and somewhat different in character. They will withstand quite low temperatures, but for safety's sake it is wise to keep this above 7°C (45°F); use a rich, open compost and place in a bright position in the greenhouse. *O. chanetii* has leaves of different lengths, greyish-green to brown, each tipped with a fine bristle. The white flowers with reddish markings appear in the form of a dense pyramidal panicle. *O. spinosa* has a much greater resemblance to *Sempervivum,* having a rosette of wedge-shaped leaves tipped with a fine bristle and a panicle of yellow flowers.

Pachycereus CACTACEAE

This is a spectacular genus with one outstanding and very popular species, *P. pringlei.* At all stages in its life it proves fascinating and attractive. It is a columnar plant, the main stem being generally rather short, but the branches can grow to great lengths (in habitat it is not unusual to see plants 12 m (40 ft) high). Plants have about fifteen ribs, very large areoles with brown felt, and many spines. Flowers only occur on mature specimens, these being whitish, about 8 cm (3 in) long. It is essentially a plant for a sunny position. Watering can be freely carried out during the growing season, but must be withheld in the rest period. A coarse, sandy soil is advantageous with humus added. It is native to many parts of lower California, the mainland of Mexico and some of the offshore islands in the Bay of California.

Pelargonium lobatum is one of the few yellow-flowering plants of the genus.

Pelargonium sibthorpiaefolium is a stem succulent, uncommon in cultivation.

Rebutia heliosa is sometimes considered 'difficult' on its own roots and subsequently grafted (as the picture depicts). It offsets freely so that eventually the developing offsets will completely obliterate the 'stock' graft.

P. weberi is a tree-like species which can reach 10 m (33 ft) in height in its native surroundings. The dark bluish-green stems are themselves a feature. They have a few radial spines rarely exceeding 2 cm ($\frac{3}{4}$ in) long and a single central to about 10 cm (4 in) in length, almost black in colour. Flowers are yellowish-white, to about 10 cm (4 in) long. They are found around Oaxaca in Mexico. *P. pecten-aboriginum* is from Sonora in more northerly Mexico. It can attain 10 m (33 ft) tall with stout branches and bears nocturnal flowers of white and pinkish shades about 8 cm (3 in) long. It gets it name from the fact that the Indian natives used the very spiny fruits as combs!

Pachyphytum CRASSULACEAE

This is a relatively small genus with thickened leaves, often in the form of an elongated rosette. *P. oviferum* has very fleshy, whitish, obovate leaves, and because of this it is referred to as the sugar almond plant. These form a thick but small rosette at intervals along the stems and branches; flowers are bell-shaped and pendent, reddish in colour. *P. hookeri* has short, cylindrical leaves, somewhat angled, pale green, and generally larger-growing than some of the species. Many pinkish flowers are produced on a rather elongated stem. *P. brevifolium* is distinctive on account of its sticky stems and wide, flat leaves. All are native to Mexico. So long as a dry season is respected, they present no problem in growing, and will suit both house or greenhouse, but a bright position is necessary. The leaves from the flowering stems can be used for propagation; a light touch will detach them, then set these in sand for rooting.

Pachypodium APOCYNACEAE

Very few groups of succulents have created so great an interest as plants of this genus. They are all stem succulents, many developing a bottle-shaped trunk, and such develop tree-like proportions. Leaves are mostly deciduous or, to say the least, short-lived, often appearing around the top of the stem in almost rosette form. They are not necessarily easy in cultivation – a temperature of at least 13°C (55°F) must be maintained at all times for successful growth. They may be propagated successfully from seeds. *P. lamerei* from southern Madagascar is quite well-known and occasionally offered as a houseplant. It can attain well over 4 m (13 ft) in height and has a barrel-shaped trunk (or caudex). As a young plant the caudex is greenish-brown and this is topped by an almost symmetrical rosette of green leaves 8 cm (3 in) or more long. Flowers will not develop until the plant is about 10 years old, then blooms about 5 cm (2 in) long will appear – these are white. *P. geayi* is somewhat similar – this also has a swollen, bottle-shaped caudex and will eventually develop tree-like proportions. The leaves are longer and narrower and eventually white flowers may be in evidence. These and others, such as *P. saundersii* with pinkish flowers and *P. densiflorum* with bright yellow flowers, are connoisseur's plants – and quickly capture the imagination.

Parodia CACTACEAE

Quite a large genus of good, fairly easily grown and flowering plants, all native to the southern parts of South America. They are mostly globular plants with distinct ribs, woolly areoles and brightly coloured spines; the majority flower at an early stage. Very good as a greenhouse plant, it can also be useful for the home if a really sunny position can be assured. Water carefully at all times, but give none when dormant. A very rich, open soil is required; regular fertilizing during the growing season can help produce excellent results. *P. chrysacanthion* is one of the better-known species, and deservedly sought after. The many ribs are divided into tubercles, each areole bearing numerous golden-yellow spines, almost covering the whole body of the plant. Woolly buds develop in the crown, opening to bright yellow flowers. *P. sanguiniflora* is a popular, deep-red flowered species. The body is fresh-green, globose, with spirally arranged, cone-shaped tubercles and many areoles with reddish-brown hooked spines. There are many to choose from, all of equal beauty, but unless due care is given to watering they might prove temperamental.

Pelargonium GERANIACEAE

A very well known group of plants, a number of which are true succulents. They are more or less shrubby succulents with fleshy leaves, stems or rootstock. All require a porous soil so that roots never become waterlogged – most flower early in the the the year. *P. lobatum* from S. Africa has a large rough, fleshy tuberous root, leaves slightly hairy and flowers of brownish-black edged with yellow. *P. sibthorpiaefolium* comes from near the mouth of the Orange River and has short fleshy stems, slightly pubescent leaves and pale pinkish-white flowers. *P. acetosum* is quite a shrubby species with slender stems and branches and oval leaves with crenated margins. Flowers of varying shades of pink in terminal clusters. These and many more are ideal subjects for either greenhouse or as houseplants, but always require a very bright position.

Pleiospilos MESEMBRYANTHEMACEAE

This genus contains over thirty species, all with varying leaf shapes and peculiarities, all clumping freely, bearing large, scented flowers. They are ideal as greenhouse subjects, but the need for a totally dry rest in dormancy is a *must*; the leaves so easily tend to rot if watered wrongly. Otherwise it is quite easy to grow if given a bright, open position. *P. simulans* is a most remarkable mimicry plant, looking like pieces of granite, the leaves being very thick, greyish-green in colour, and flattened on the inner surface. It groups very readily and produces large, golden-yellow flowers. Very similar are *P. bolusii* and *P. nelii;* the former has leaves resembling the toe of a wooden shoe, wrinkled and very granite-like. *P. nelii* is much smoother and rounded; the flowers are brownish-yellow. They easily grow from seed, producing a flowering specimen in about three years. Like most plants of this huge family, a very porous soil is needed; added humus is an advantage, but again, watering procedure is of the utmost importance. All these plants are native to South Africa.

Portulaca PORTULACACEAE

A popular genus which really needs no introduction – the hybrids of some species have become useful bedding plants in gardens around the world. Plants are native of South America and the West Indies, also southern Africa and Australia. They are mainly spreading plants by means of elongated branches – just a few prove to be semi-erect in habit. With only few exceptions they provide no difficulties in cultivation – some can be propagated by cuttings, but all respond very well to growing from seeds. *P. grandiflora* was a species originally described botanically by the famous botanist, Hooker. This species is now rather difficult to locate in the wild, but it does still inhabit some of the Windward Islands of the

Caribbean. A low growing plant with almost cylindrical leaves which are fleshy and minutely hairy and arranged alternate along the trailing stems. Flowers are borne from the terminal ends of the spreading branches, reddish-pink in colour. This is one of the parents of the plants grown in gardens – these hybrids offering plants with flowers of red, yellow, orange, purple and white. *P. hawaiiensis,* as its name suggests, is from Hawaii. This has a very fleshy rootstock, with fleshy stems and branches to 20 cm (8 in) long. Leaves are more or less oval and quite thick, and in the leaf axils long orange-reddish hairs appear. Flowers are red and white, about 2 cm ($\frac{3}{4}$ in) across. *P. decipiens* is a species 8–13 cm tall with a number of fleshy branches. The leaves are almost cylindrical and very slender to about 1.2 cm ($\frac{1}{2}$ in) long. This also has brownish hairs in the leaf axils, about 4 mm ($\frac{1}{8}$ in) long. Flowers are small, almost cup-shaped, pale yellow in colour. This is found in several areas of Australia.

Pterodiscus PEDALIACEAE
Only a few species are involved, originating from South Africa or Namibia. The most spectacular is *P. speciosus,* a small fleshy-stemmed plant which gradually develops a thick, almost bottle-shaped, base to the stem. The leaves appear near the top of the plant with a profusion of purplish-pink flowers. Others of the genus include *P. luridus* with yellowish flowers covered with reddish dots. They are not difficult to grow, requiring a minimum temperature of 10°C (50°F) even during the resting period when they lose their foliage.

Rathbunia CACTACEAE
This is a small genus of clambering, elongated plants native to more northerly areas of Mexico. Whilst they have a sprawling habit and form clusters, they are quite interesting when young. *R. alamosensis* is the best-known species – stem growth is columnar, with five to eight distinct ribs, and areoles bearing straight and spreading greyish spines. Flowers are rich scarlet, sometimes up to 10 cm (4 in) in length, followed by large, globular red fruits containing many seeds. Suitable for the greenhouse where a bright position should be provided; soil needs to be quite rich for best results, but decidedly open and porous, and it must be kept completely dry during the rest season.

Rebutia CACTACEAE
This is another of the most popular genera, consisting of many species of small growth and generally of grouping habit. One of the easiest groups to grow – only few present any problem – their flowers, in all their vivid colourings, are the ultimate rewarding feature. *R. minuscula* is frequently seen, having bright-green, globular stems, many low ribs consisting of

small, rounded tubercles and areoles with very small, white spines. It is always of clustering habit, producing many bright red flowers; it is native to Argentina. *R. marsoneri* has dark green, rounded stems, readily grouping, the spines being short and brownish-yellow; flowers are yellow. This species is also native to Argentina. *R. senilis* has a dense coat of white, bristle-like spines and rich, carmine-red flowers; *var. kesselringiana* has very similar appearance, but with yellow flowers. Other flower colourings can be provided by this versatile genus: white with the somewhat miniature, whitish-spined *R. albiflora;* or deep pink with *R. kariusiana* with its deeper green body and slightly larger growth. *R. heliosa* is a unique plant, a Bolivian species with very short spines set in comb-like formation. Its flowers are orange or orange-yellow with a whitish centre. Plants are suitable for greenhouse or home, but a not too sunny position is recommended. Soil must be rich and porous, with regular watering throughout the growing season; periodic fertilizing will help to maintain the production of flowers over a long period. Plants are easily grown from seeds taking only a year or two to flower.

Rhipsalidopsis CACTACEAE
Well-known plants of a small genus, they are usually known as Easter cactus due to their period of flowering. Species are epiphytic, but flourish well as pot plants so long as the soil is rich in humus, reasonably porous, and never allowed to completely dry out, hence a minimum temperature of 10°C (50°F) should be maintained. *R. rosea* is rather a small, shrub-like plant, inclined to have pendent stems of small, flattish, slightly pink-tinted, flat, oval segments. Flowers are rose-pink, appearing in early to late spring. It is native to Southern Brazil. *R. gaertneri* was for a long time included in the genus *Schlumbergera,* and this is the very rewarding Easter cactus. Stems are dark, shiny but green in colour, sometimes with slightly purplish markings on the margins. Flowers develop from the tips of the joints, being bright red to scarlet. These species are very much house plants, but are equally successful in the greenhouse; a shady position is required as too much sun can quickly dehydrate these plants. A short resting period, immediately after flowering, is advised.

Rhipsalis CACTACEAE
A very large and varied genus of epiphytic plants, their stems take on many forms – twisted, angled, flattened, slender to quite thick pencil-like. It is still considered a somewhat confusing group and often it is difficult to decide correct nomenclature. All plants must be grown in shady conditions and they are well suited for hanging-basket work as their stems and branches are of pendent habit. Soil should be rich, porous and never allowed to become completely dry, with a minimum

temperature of 10°C (50°F). They are easily propagated by stem cuttings – a bushy specimen is a joy to behold! *R. capilliformis* represents the very fine pencil-shaped, elongated stem species – very delicate and graceful and a picture when covered with numerous small creamy-white flowers. *R. cereuscula* has slightly thicker, rounded stems and branches, elongated with massed branching at the stem terminals. Flowers are creamy-pink. *R. shaferi* has even thicker and purplish-green stems, somewhat more rigid, but still of pendent habit. Flowers are white or greenish-white. This species is native to Brazil. *R. cereiodes* has triangular-sectioned stems, with either short or longish joints with hard margins and bearing pure white flowers. Several species have flattened stems; those of *R. bolivianus* are strap-like, very similar to the *Lepismium* in shape and colouring. *R. platycarpa* is a much-branched species with somewhat elongated, flattened joints, dark green, with margins crenated. It produces many creamy-yellow flowers to an areole, and then white fruits. *R. paradoxa* (now referred to as *Lepismium paradoxum*) has peculiar link-like stems and branches, developing in whorls. Flower and fruit are white. There are several more deserving mention; perhaps *R. houlletiana* is of particular consequence having flat, leaf-like stems developing from a thin, slender 'stalk', almost terete. The fresh green of the stems, with their pronounced crenated margins, and subsequently the host of quite large creamy flowers make this one of the best species, and the purple fruits offer a very desirable 'extra'. If there is any genus in the family Cactaceae which offers something different, then it is surely *Rhipsalis* – and in addition, they are easy to grow.

Ruschia MESEMBRYANTHEMACEAE
This is a very large genus of well over 300 species, all somewhat shrubby in habit, and the larger-growing species are mainly easier to grow than the small ones, so care must be taken in selecting your plants. *R. karrooica* is a quite sizeable, fleshy-leaved plant, having numerous, slender, low-growing, then ascending branches, from which are produced opposite leaves, the bases of which form a sheath around the stem, the sheath meeting the next lower pair of leaves. *R. acuminata* is very similar, growth-wise, the main attraction being the beautiful white flowers, as fine as are found on any of the species. They require a very open soil, moderate watering at all times, and a minimum temperature of 10°C (50°F). They all benefit from full sun, and are suitable for the house or greenhouse so long as all cultural requirements are met.

Sansevieria AGAVACEAE
This is a well-known genus which includes plants long-used as house plants. It is nevertheless a fairly large group, many of which are exceed-

ingly difficult to obtain, and likewise not too easy to grow. However, some are worth mentioning, and can certainly be considered of easy culture. *S. trifasciata var. laurentii* is the popular mother-in-law's tongue; its sword-like leaves are erect and marked with yellow marginal lines and whitish crossbands. It comes from tropical Africa and has spikes of white flowers. There is also a very interesting sport of this species, *S. hahnii,* which has the habit of a close rosette and clusters freely. The leaves are dark green with pale green crossbands. In more recent times a spectacular variegated form has been developed, with many yellow lines and markings. There are several others which are equally fascinating but they are not readily available. Be sure never to over-water as they hate it!

Sarcocaulon GERANIACEAE
These are rather low-growing shrubby plants with solitary flowers; if they are kept dry they remain leafless, but given water they will bear numerous small, bright green leaves. It is wise to provide a minimum temperature of 10°C (50°F) as flowers often appear quite early in the year. An open, fairly rich soil is advisable, and seemingly full sun or semi-shade is equally good for flowering. The driest period of the year for them should be early autumn to early winter. *S. burmannii* has thick, gnarled, often spiny, greyish-green branches, resembling a bonsai, bearing pinkish-white flowers. *S. rigidum* has spiny stems and branches, spreading horizontally, leaves with two lobes, flowers with narrow petals, deep pink to reddish in colour. These are all native to South Africa or Namibia and offer splendid scope for the 'unusual' either indoors or in the greenhouse.

Sarcostemma ASCLEPIADACEAE
This is a rather small genus of large-growing, vine-like plants, all of comparatively easy growth, but somewhat uninteresting in appearance. *S. viminale* has thin cylindrical branches, these being firstly semi-erect, then pendent, jointed by greyish-green triangular leaf scales. The small white flowers are borne in umbels. A reasonably warm temperature is necessary at all times, together with a compost fairly rich in humus. Sun is possibly best, but so long as good light is afforded, plants appear to flourish.

Schlumbergera CACTACEAE
This is a genus which has, together with *Zygocactus*, been the subject of much research and taxonomic change during the past years. It has lost the popular Easter cactus, *Schlumbergera gaertneri* (now *Rhipsalidopsis*) and gained the Christmas cactus, *Zygocactus truncatus*. *S. truncatus* is actually the species, and one of the parents of the Christmas cactus, the latter being a hybrid between *S. truncatus* and *S. russelliana*. Therefore it must

A very suitable item for a hanging-basket – a true epiphyte, *Rhipsalis pachyptera* produces leaf-like segmented stems and yellowish-white flowers from the areoles.

be accepted that what we admire during the Christmas season is *not* the true species. The flower bears a strong resemblance, but the joints are definitely different; the species has toothed segments (typical of all those originally included in *Zygocactus*) not the rounded joints invariably found. This is, of course, a splendid houseplant and also suited for green-house culture. Keep a good temperature, a semi-shaded position, and never allow the plant to go completely dry. The compost should be rich and porous; regular fertilizing during the flowering season is more than justified. One other factor: once the plants come into bud, do not change their position. If you do, the tendency is for bud-drop. There are several varieties and cultivars, all well worth acquiring: *var. delicatus* is not too easy to grow, but the white flowers are exceedingly beautiful; cv 'Noris' has rounded flower segments, magenta with red-orange; cv 'Lilac Beauty' is a remarkably pretty plant, the flowers having a white centre surrounded by lilac-purple. For the record, the typical Christmas cactus is now called *S.* 'Bridgesii'.

Another genus, *Epiphyllanthus*, has more recently been merged with *Schlumbergera*. These very uncommon plants have thick fleshy joints with minute spines more reminiscent of miniature *Opuntia* species. *S. opuntioides* is the best known, with pale to deep purple flowers similar in shape to other *Schlumbergeras*.

Scilla LILIACEAE

Some species of this well-known genus are considered succulents; it is indeed very difficult to draw a line of demarcation as to which are, and which are not! *S. violacea* is small-growing, the stems having a very swollen base, and it clusters freely. Leaves are perennial, fleshy, olive-green on the upper surface, reddish-brown on lower. Flowers are bluish. *S. socialis* has a much larger bulbous base, offsetting freely and having short, dark-green, broad and fleshy leaves with many paler blotches on the upper surface. Flowers are greenish-blue. All such species enjoy a fairly high temperature and will continue growing throughout much of the year if moisture is made available. A bright, but not directly sunny position is most suitable, with rich, porous soil. Fertilize during the flowering season. They are useful for either greenhouse or home culture.

Sedum CRASSULACEAE

A large genus of popular plants, very widespread in its distribution – Europe, Asia, Africa and America. Their variety is certainly the keynote! Plants range from miniatures with small, bead-like leaves, to large, fleshy-stemmed shrubby species, and with very few exceptions can be considered excellent plants for the beginner. To some degree cultural requirements might vary, but overall the majority of species can be accommodated in a very sandy or gritty compost, the main essential being that the mixture must be porous otherwise rot can set in without warning. Those most frequently encountered prefer a bright, sunny position, especially where leaf coloration is one of the pleasing aspects. Moderate watering can be continued throughout the year, but do not let the temperature drop too much. *S. hintonii* is one of the prettiest species, originating from Mexico. Leaves are rounded, pale green and densely covered with fine, minute white hairs, and are formed as a rosette. With careful growing it clusters quite freely, producing white flowers. Careful watering is essential (see pp. 20–1). *S. multiceps*, from Algeria, is an interesting plant, the growth resembling small pine trees. *S. sieboldii* is of Japanese origin, and can be considered completely hardy, although, unfortunately, it is deciduous, Leaves are flat, roundish and notched, often edged pink or brown. There is also a very attractive variegated form. Both are suited for hanging baskets. Another eye-catching Japanese species is *S. spectabile*, well known as a hardy garden plant for many years; its spectacular growth and flower make this one of the finest species, the leaves being large, thick and fleshy, bluish-grey in colour. Flowers are an added bonus, with numerous large heads of bright pink; the petals are particularly long, as also are the stamens. *S. frutescens* is a miniature, tree-like plant, native to Southern Mexico; the stem is very thick with papery bark, flat bright-green leaves and masses of small white flowers. *S. brevifolium*, from Morocco, forms cushions of small, white leaves flushed red and carries white flowers. Altogether it is difficult to exclude any species from this record as there is such a vast range and it is hard to find a disappointment amongst the 500 or so species!

Selenicereus CACTACEAE

It is necessary to have ample room for species of this genus; all are climbing or clambering plants, with slender, elongated stems and branches, and mainly nocturnal flowers. Many glamorous names have been passed to these species on account of their large, fragrant, beautiful flowers; queen of the night, princess of the night, moonflower, etc. *S. grandiflorus* is from the West Indies, having large exotic white flowers 23 cm (9 in) in diameter. Even larger is *S. pteranthus* from Mexico with flowers up to 30 cm (12 in) in diameter. Several others are commonly found in collections and all are quite easy to grow, but keep the soil rich and porous for best results. It is also wise to remember that most are from forest areas, resulting in their roots being in the shade, and their stems and branches clambering up the trees to the daylight above. Water must always be administered with care, and during the coldest months is best omitted. Rooted cuttings of *S. macdonaldii* are often used for grafting purposes.

Sempervivum CRASSULACEAE

This is another well-known genus of reasonably hardy plants, mostly of European origin. This is, of course, the family of houseleeks; all the species have beautifully marked and fashioned rosettes with quite spectacular flowers, and all are of grouping habit. *S. arachnoideum* has small rosettes, with fine webs of hairs from tip to tip of the leaves. Flowers are pinkish or reddish. *S. tectorum* has many varietal forms; this is the typical houseleek with ovate, grey-green leaves, tipped red, and clusters of reddish or greenish flowers. Cultivation presents no difficulties; the majority are totally frost-resistant, will take water at any time, and will cluster to produce large mats, seemingly more so if they have an elevated position where good drainage is available. Any ordinary porous soil appears suitable, but do not grow in shade as they easily become etiolated and unshapely.

Senecio COMPOSITAE

This is another huge genus which includes a great number of succulent species, many of rather extraordinary growth and flower. The African species are possibly the most interesting and provide the greater range of variation and characteristics. *S. scaposus* forms loose rosettes of slender, pencil-like leaves, covered with a felt coating; just below the tip of each leaf is a small flattened area. Flowers are yellow, but rather uninteresting. *S. haworthii* has erect stems and branches with cylindrical, pointed leaves, all parts of the plant being covered by a white, almost woolly coating. Flowers are yellow. These plants demand an open soil, a reasonably bright position, and good watering in the growing season. They are generally adaptable to either the greenhouse or home culture, especially the latter as young plants.

Setiechinopsis CACTACEAE

This is a somewhat disputed genus, now considered more appropriately synonymous with *Arthrocereus*. However it contains one very popular and well-known species which demands its inclusion in this record. *S. mirabilis* is a somewhat smallish plant, cylindrical in shape, about 15 cm (6 in) high, the stem being dull greyish-yellowish-green in colour; it has areoles with many slender spines. The white flowers are borne on a long tube from near the apex. It is of Argentinian origin. The greenhouse is the better home for the plant, in a fairly bright position, completely dry during dormancy and with free watering in the growing season; the soil must be rich in humus for best results, and porous.

Stapelia ASCLEPIADACEAE

This is a very large genus of fascinating species with mostly attractive flowers, which sometimes carry an obnoxious smell – hence certain are termed carrion flower. In recent years the genus has been reclassified with some species now included under the resurrected generic title of *Orbea*. Whilst a few are of reasonably easy culture, there are others which provide considerable difficulty, so it is wise to know more about a particular plant and its requirements before purchasing. They are, by nature, native to semi-arid regions; thus they are able to tolerate long periods of drought; generous watering can be the cause of many disappointments and problems. A bright, airy position is essential, but full sun can prove harmful to their appearance. They must be considered 'greedy' plants, needing a very rich, but very sandy compost and frequent fertilizing during the growing season. A long, completely dry, dormancy is needed and even then it is unwise to allow temperatures to fall below 10°C (50°F). Watering should only be commenced when there is certainty of continued warmth and sunshine.

S. *variegata (Orbea variegata)*is the most popular of all, clustering readily with stems to about 10 cm (4 in) long, angled with spreading teeth and showy flowers, greenish-yellow with purplish-brown spots, lobes wrinkled with many transverse lines, and, unfortunately, ill-smelling! *S. gettleffii* has bright green stems, edged with quite long rudimentary leaves, and flowers of variable shades of cream to pale lemon-yellow, banded with purple stripes. *S. comparabilis* has very distinctly succulent stems, often to 2 cm ($\frac{3}{4}$ in) thick, four-angled and toothed. Flowers grow to about 10 cm (4 in) in diameter, rounded, starlike and very hairy, basically brownish-purple with slightly wavy, yellowish transverse lines. *S. asterias* has dark-green, silky, four-angled stems, of erect growth and quickly forms clusters. Flowers are very star-like with long, brownish-red lobes and transverse bands. *S. hirsuta* can easily be confused with the previous species; stems are quite similar, with large, reddish-yellow lobes, purplish-red transverse lines and purplish hairs along the margins.

Among the largest flowering species are *S. grandiflora* with dark-brown lobes and hairy margins often 15 cm (6 in) in diameter; *S. flavirostris* distinguished by the unusual yellow colouring of the inner corona and the banding of the corolla lobes with transverse lines; and *S. gigantea* with stout, angled stems growing to about 20 cm (8 in) long, small teeth on the angles, dull velvety-green in colour and huge, pale yellow flowers 35 cm (14 in) in diameter having many undulating, reddish transverse lines. Perhaps one of the most fascinating species is *S. clavicorona* which has erect shoots up to 30 cm (12 in) tall, soft, velvety green and distinctly four-angled. Flowers are brownish-grey, their rounded lobes covered with thin reddish-purple transverse lines. The selection is vast, but never assume all are as easy to cultivate as *S. variegata*. Nevertheless, success can be achieved if due care is taken. They are mostly suited to greenhouse culture, and all are native to South Africa.

Stapelianthus ASCLEPIADACEAE

A rather small genus of Madagascan succulents closely related to *Huernia*. They are clump-forming plants with mostly angular stems and branches. *S. pilosus* develops very thick clumps of green or purplish-brown stems which root as they spread over the surface of the ground. Flowers are somewhat bell-shaped, fleshy, yellowish with maroon-red blotches. *S. insignis* has four-angled, reddish-grey stems blotched and marked with a darker colouring. Flowers are almost globular, pale reddish-green externally and blotched maroon – whitish on the inner surface and heavily blotched with very deep maroon. This is one of the most fascinating genera within Asclepiadaceae.

Stenocereus CACTACEAE

This fairly large genus has recently absorbed several others such as *Lemaireocereus, Hertrichocereus* and *Marginatocereus*. All species are

Selenicereus macdonaldii has a huge nocturnal flower measuring nearly 30 cm (12 in) in diameter and sweetly scented.

columnar or tree-forming plants and present no difficulty in cultivation. Flowers are usually nocturnal and invariably quite large. *S. stellatus* has reddish-dark-green stems, fairly spiny and bearing pure white terminal flowers whose petals are pinkish externally. *S. marginatus* is also tall growing, almost tree-like in maturity, with white to brown areoles with large white flowers, reddish on the outside. *S. thurberi* Buxb. is found in S. Arizona in U.S.A. and Sonora, Mexico. It is a tall-growing species, freely branching from the base with erect deep-green, very erect growth which has won it the common title of Organ-pipe Cactus. The stems tend to develop a bluish tinge with maturity – they can reach 5–6 m ($16\frac{1}{2}$–20 ft) tall – about 20 cm (8 in) wide, with up to 19 ribs. Radial spines about 7 in number, 1 cm ($\frac{3}{8}$ in) long, one or more centrals about twice as long – all brownish-black. Flowers are white about 6 cm ($2\frac{1}{2}$ in) long with a pinkish centre. Other species include *S. dumortieri*, another tree-like plant, and *S. beneckei*, both of which are from Mexico, readily available and of very easy culture, and, although tree-like in habitat, are unlikely to exceed 1 m ($3\frac{1}{4}$ ft) in cultivation. Over 20 species are recorded of much the same habit. They are native to the more central regions of America.

Stetsonia CACTACEAE
A monotypic genus of great attraction, particularly when the plants are young. Of erect growth, in maturity the plants develop tree-like characteristics. *S. coryne* is very well-known, the pale-green stems having seven to nine obtuse ribs, woolly areoles bearing long, slender, greyish-black spines of unequal length and, when mature, white flowers on a long tube, opening at night. It is known only from north-west Argentina. This presents little difficulty in cultivation. It is easily reared from seeds and very suitable for indoor culture, such as bowl gardens when young, or equally at home in the greenhouse. A good, bright position is required, a rather short rest period in the coldest weather, and generous watering as the weather improves. A rich soil will encourage better growth and vigour, but keep the mixture porous.

Stomatium MESEMBRYANTHEMACEAE
This comprises about forty low-growing, very attractively shaped leaf succulents which readily form clusters and bear fragrant, nocturnal flowers. In many ways they resemble *Faucaria,* but the leaves are much smaller, with rather blunt tips, and short teeth on the margins, generally greyish-green in colour. Ideally suited for home or greenhouse, they require good open compost, a bright position and careful watering, especially in the colder months. Flowers appear in the late spring or early

summer, when temperatures must be maintained at not less than 13°C (55°F); higher if possible. All are native to South Africa. It is rather difficult to appreciate the differences between some of the species, although, together, these become more apparent. All are easily grown, and quickly form dwarf clusters, even from seeds or cuttings. The best known are *S. fulleri,* which has pronounced whitish warts on the lower surface of its leaves; and *S. agninum,* with boatshaped leaves, flat on the upper surface, convex and keeled on the under surface. Both these species have yellow flowers, as also do *S. jamesii, S. meyeri* and *S. ronaldii. S. alboroseum* is one of the few exceptions having white flowers.

Sulcorebutia CACTACEAE

A very popular genus of rather small-growing species of clustering habit, with very pronounced areoles and extraordinarily colourful flowers. They were introduced into cultivation not long ago from Bolivia, and at first were thought to be somewhat difficult to grow on their own roots, the result being that they were grafted to encourage their survival. In some ways they are slow to grow on their own roots, and for this reason grafting is advisable, but it is not essential. Their culture requires careful attention: definitely a rich, open soil, essentially a sunny position, and watering only when the growing season has commenced and weather conditions permit. *S. steinbachii* is small, globular, and caespitose with a dark green body, tuberculate ribs, somewhat elongated narrow areoles and spreading brown spines; flowers are a deep rich-red. *S. glomeriseta* is densely covered with numerous whitish bristly spines from small elongated narrow areoles, and bears bright yellow flowers. *S. rauschii* is undoubtedly one of the most distinctive, with a blackish-green-grey body, ribs divided into round flattened tubercles, and the typical narrow areoles with close-set, small, black spines. The flowers are a beautiful magenta-rose with a white throat. There are several other species to select from, and without exception they are rewarding plants to grow for they have such variety of rich colouring in their flowers. So long as due attention is given to their needs, and preferably a minimum temperature of 13°C (55°F) is provided, successful results can be achieved.

Thelocactus CACTACEAE

This is yet another genus with colourful flowers which merits much greater popularity. Only one species, *T. bicolor* has really put itself in the front-line of popularity, and this is in many ways resembles a smaller growing species of *Ferocactus.* Its conical stems are broadly ribbed and tubercled, the pronounced areoles have colourful reddish, brownish or yellowish spines and quite large purplish-pink flowers. They originate from Texas to central Mexico, and certain varietal differences occur according to habitat. However, other species can provide equally attractive characteristics and offer no greater problems in cultivation. *T. conothele* and its variety *aurantiacus* is a well known, colourful and easily flowered species. *T. lophothele* has a depressed crown, slender ribs and distinct tubercles. Areoles bear a few, yellowish, curved spines and pale yellow flowers. *T. nidulans* is an much sought-after species, very different in many respects from the previously mentioned. It comes from the central areas of Mexico, and can be as much as 20 cm (8 in) in diameter, silvery or bluish-grey in colour, many wavy ribs divided into tubercles, and the areoles carrying shredding silvery-white spines and yellowish-white flowers. Others could be mentioned and can be recommended; all are suitable for greenhouse culture. Their main demand is a very sunny position, a moderately rich, open soil, careful watering at all times and none whatsoever in the coldest months when the soil must be kept completely dry; they will then accept as low a temperature as 7°C (45°F) without coming to harm.

Titanopsis MESEMBRYANTHEMACEAE
A small genus, it contains well-known and popular species, all having peculiar and attractive leaf forms and markings. They are dwarf-growing plants which cluster freely, with flowers borne on long stalks. In general they are not too difficult to grow; overwatering can prove the biggest danger as this might cause them to lose their leaf characteristics and possibly set up rot. Firstly a very sunny and bright position must be assured; next, the soil must be open and contain a percentage of lime since they inhabit limestone areas in their natural habitat; finally, exercise care in watering, keeping completely dry in coldest months. *T. calcarea* is very well-known; the leaves resemble small pieces of limestone, being greyish, flattish and covered with whitish-grey tubercles and set in the form of a rosette; flowers are yellow. *T. setifera* is also distinctive and different, the leaves being thicker and greener, with not such prominent tubercles on the tips, but small teeth on the edges and both surfaces, leaves arranged rosette-wise. These form very exciting and unusual items for the greenhouse. All are native to South Africa.

Tradescantia COMMELINACEAE
This is a large family of popular plants, many of which are semi-succulent, but here only one species is considered. *T. navicularis* is a creeping species, with stems divided into short segments. Leaves are fleshy, somewhat boat-shaped, set in two ranks, greyish-green on the upper surface and reddish on the under surface. Flowers are purplish-pink. This is a curiosity rather than an attractive plant but it provides no problem in cultivation; perhaps a little more moisture should be given than to most succulents during

One of the taller growing species of the genus, *Stapelia clavicorona* has stems to about 30 cm (12 in) long, sturdy and four-angled with flowers possessing a unique charm.

dormancy, and that only to avoid shrivelling of the leaves. An open, fairly rich compost is advised in a semi-shady position, and ample space to spread around. It is easily propagated from cuttings.

Trichodiadema MESEMBRYANTHEMACEAE

These are mostly shrubby plants with peculiar leaves having spine-like bristles on the leaf-tips; the generic title means crown of bristles. They are all of South African origin and present no difficulties in cultivation, but it should be ensured that the soil is kept porous and watering should be withheld in the rest period. All are easy flowering, and colourings range from white to deepest reddish-purple. *T. densum* is one of the best known of the genus, the spines giving it a very cactus-like appearance. Growth comes from quite a thick root system; the stems are short and densely covered with the bristly leaves, the bristles having white tips. Flowers are reddish-purple. *T. bulbosum* is very similar, but more sprawling in habit; the flowers are of similar colouring. *T. mirabile* has a compact, low-growing habit, the little bristles being more erect, and the flowers white. There are possibly over thirty species in the genus; all are suitable for a bright sunny position in the home or the greenhouse.

Turbinocarpus CACTACEAE

An interesting genus of comparatively small-growing cacti, it is not very common in cultivation, but does not present difficulties in growing so long as basic needs are met. All species require a sunny, bright position, and undoubtedly the greenhouse is the best choice. *T. lophophoroides* is bluish-grey in colour, globular in shape, rarely with spines, and bears large, whitish-pink flowers. *T. polaskii* is very similar, but somewhat smaller, and has a few soft, curved spines and large pink-and-white flowers.

T. valdezianus will long be remembered as *Pelecyphora valdezianus*. It is one of the choice miniatures which will always claim the enthusiasm of the collector. The body measures only about 2.5 cm (1 in) high and wide – dark greyish-green in colour with many greyish-white areoles densely set with numerous feathery, hair-like, radial spines barely exceeding 1 mm long. Flowers are about 2 cm ($\frac{3}{4}$ in) across – pale reddish-purple or sometimes pure white, appearing from around the crown of the plant. This is a mountain plant from Coahuila, Mexico. *P. pseudopectinata* is another fairly small species from Tamaulipas, Mexico. It measures about 6 cm (2$\frac{1}{2}$ in) tall and 4 cm (1$\frac{1}{2}$ in) wide, with tubercles spirally arranged – these have small areoles which bear small white spines arranged in a comb-like setting. Flowers are about 2 cm ($\frac{3}{4}$ in) long and 3 cm (1$\frac{1}{4}$ in) across, white with a pinkish median line on each petal, sometimes reddish-purple.

Other species include: *T. schmiedickeanus* which has a dark, grey-green body and many tubercles, and at the apex a tuft of quite long, thick, slightly curved spines with pale pink flowers and deeper markings; *T. macrochele* and *T. pseudomacrochele* which are also worthwhile, and, along with any of this genus, will offer a pleasing and somewhat unique feature. All species are from Mexico.

Villadia CRASSULACEAE

A small genus of clambering plants, strongly reminiscent of many of the *Sedum* species, all native of high altitudes from Central Mexico to Peru. They present no difficulties in growing; once established they will look after themselves, but even so, it is best to be careful.

V. batesii from Central Mexico has stems to 15 cm (6 in) long, greenish-red. Leaves are cylindrical, covered with numerous minute 'warts' – these leaves, each about 1 cm ($\frac{3}{8}$ in) long form a neat rosette at the tips of the stems. Flowers are pinkish-red in a flattened cluster on a short stalk. *V. virgata* is, as are the following species, a native of Peru. This is a small bushy species with erect stems and branches – often to 25 cm (10 in) tall. Leaves deep-green, ovate, about 6 mm ($\frac{1}{4}$ in) long and 2 mm ($\frac{1}{16}$ in) wide – very fleshy. Flowers are whitish, borne on a slender spike.

V. berillonana has short stems with greyish-green leaves, very fleshy and almost circular. Flowers are yellow, carried on a long stalk. Perhaps the most startling is *V. andina* which is of low growth, and clusters freely; the stems and leaves are very succulent, the latter being quite small and semi-globose in shape. Flowers are almost black-red, on short stalks.

Weingartia CACTACEAE

This genus is closely linked, botanically, with *Sulcorebutia* and *Gymnocalycium,* and, like these, is native to South America. The distinctive feature is the turnip-shaped root. They make good greenhouse subjects, needing plenty of light and a very porous compost. They should be kept completely dry in winter and only very moderately watered at any other time. Flowers are produced very freely. *W. fidaiana,* from Bolivia, has a globular stem, with pronounced woolly areoles and yellowish-brown spines; it is generally more miniature-growing than others of the genus. Flowers are bright orange-yellow. *W. torotorensis* has distinctive tubercles with numerous yellowish spines and rose-pink flowers. These are plants which may require seeking after; specialist nurseries may be the best source to try, but the results will justify the effort!

Wilcoxia CACTACEAE

These are very unusual desert plants with tuberous roots and mainly

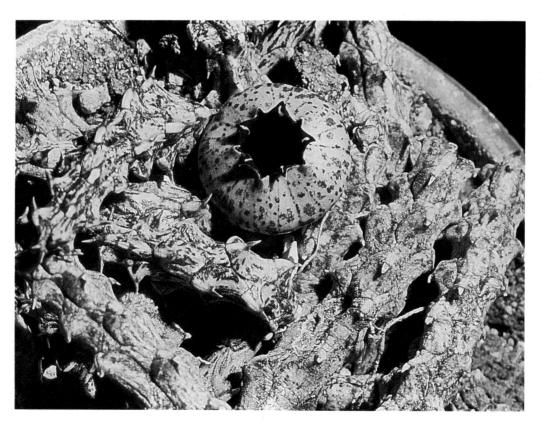

Stapelianthus insignis has a remarkably fascinating, flask-shaped flower borne from low-growing, spreading greenish-brown branches.

longish, slender, erect stems and colourful, attractive flowers. Recent reclassification has moved most of these species into *Echinocereus*, but because of their unusual characteristics, as well as their popularity, they are here kept separate. Complete dryness during the coldest months is very necessary, and even in the growing season great care should be exercised with regard to watering; these plants not only store moisture in their stems, but also their roots, and over-watering can easily cause rot. These are best suited for the greenhouse and should have a sunny position, porous soil with some lime added, and periodic fertilizing as the flower buds appear. *W. poselgeri* is the best known species, and has long, slender greyish-green stems, extremely minute spines and colourful pinkish-purple flowers, very similar to some *Echinocereus* species. *W. albiflora* has somewhat similar growth, perhaps more greyish in stem colouring, and bears almost pure white flowers. *W. schmollii* is rather different; the stems are soft, slender, and greyish-green; ribs are tuberculate and the many woolly areoles have thin, white spines. Flowers are

The red-flowering *Sulcorebutia mentosa* (*left*) is one of the many species introduced into cultivation in recent years – all are sought after and relatively easy to grow.

pinkish-purple. This is frequently offered as a grafted plant, but it grows quite successfully on its own roots. All species are native to Mexico.

Yucca AGAVACEAE

Unless ample provision can be made for their development they are very likely to outgrow their living space under glass. A few, of course, can be grown very well out-of-doors, in parts of southern England. Young plants can, however, give a pleasing appearance to a greenhouse, or, if a very sunny position is guaranteed, prove most acceptable as a feature plant in the home. If it is a matter of selecting young plants, then the choice should rest between the following: *Y. aloifolia* and its *vars. marginata* and *tricolor* (the latter two often erroneously termed *Y. aloifolia var. variegata*) and *Y. filamentosa,* the leaves of which are edged with curly white hairs. The foliage effect of each is startling, and as background plants in a greenhouse they are superb. There are no problems in growing; the biggest difficulty will be met with when the plant grows too big to be housed!